职业教育·铁道运输类专业教材

铁路客运服务英语

王媛媛　应婷婷　主　编
许　媛　刘　慧　黄　辉　副主编
夏　栋　主　审

人民交通出版社股份有限公司
北　京

内 容 提 要

本书为职业教育·铁道运输类专业教材。全书按照轨道交通客运服务作业流程进行编写，包含站厅服务、列车服务及其他服务三个部分18个教学任务，主要内容包括：问询、售票、进站、候车、检票、出站、车站广播、列车设备、迎客、车厢服务、餐车服务、列车广播、下车服务、重点旅客服务、投诉处理、失物招领、应急处理及感谢、道歉与建议。

本书为轨道交通相关专业课程教材，可供职业院校轨道交通相关专业教学使用，亦可供轨道交通行业培训使用。

本书配有教学课件，读者可通过加入职教铁路教学研讨群（教师专用QQ群号：211163250）。

图书在版编目（CIP）数据

铁路客运服务英语 / 王媛媛，应婷婷主编．— 北京：人民交通出版社股份有限公司，2020.7
ISBN 978-7-114-16423-1

Ⅰ．①铁… Ⅱ．①王… ②应… Ⅲ．①铁路运输—客运服务—英语—高等学校—教材 Ⅳ．①U293.3

中国版本图书馆 CIP 数据核字（2020）第 046269 号

职业教育·铁道运输类专业教材
书　　名：铁路客运服务英语
著 作 者：王媛媛　应婷婷
责任编辑：王　丹
责任校对：刘　芹
责任印制：刘高彤
出版发行：人民交通出版社股份有限公司
地　　址：（100011）北京市朝阳区安定门外外馆斜街3号
网　　址：http://www.ccpcl.com.cn
销售电话：(010)59757973
总 经 销：人民交通出版社股份有限公司发行部
经　　销：各地新华书店
印　　刷：北京鑫正大印刷有限公司
开　　本：787×1092　1/16
印　　张：11
字　　数：330千
版　　次：2020年7月　第1版
印　　次：2022年1月　第3次印刷
书　　号：ISBN 978-7-114-16423-1
定　　价：36.00元

（有印刷、装订质量问题的图书由本公司负责调换）

前　言

课程特点

铁路客运服务英语是铁道交通运营管理、高速铁路客运乘务、城市轨道交通运营管理等轨道交通相关专业的基础课程之一，主要学习轨道交通客运服务工作中所需要的专业英语词汇及相关表达方式，使学生具备良好的英语表达及阅读能力，达到轨道交通客运服务岗位职业标准的相关要求。

编写背景

铁路作为国民经济大动脉、关键基础设施和重大民生工程，在国民经济和社会发展中具有重要作用。交通强国，铁路先行，中国高铁"走出去"成为亮丽的国家名片。到2025年，铁路网规模将从2018年的13.1万公里增加到17.5万公里，其中高速铁路从2018年的2.9万公里增加到3.8万公里，高铁布局将从"四纵四横"发展到"八纵八横"；全国规划建设城市轨道交通的城市将从2018年的35个增加到43个，运行线路总里程从2018年的5761公里增加到8600公里。轨道交通的快速发展及国际交流合作的不断加强，急需大批具有一定英语交际能力的高端技术技能人才。本教材旨在帮助轨道交通相关专业在校学生及轨道交通行业一线服务人员熟悉轨道交通服务的英语表达方式，掌握必要的英语会话技能，提升英语交流水平，进而提高服务质量，助力中国高铁"走出去"。

内容结构

本书共分为3部分，第1部分为站厅服务，根据地点的不同划分为7个单元，分别介绍问询、售票、进站、候车、检票、出站和车站广播的相关英语表达方式。第2部分为列车服务，包含6个单元，分别介绍列车设备、迎客、车厢服务、餐车服务、列车广播、下车服务的相关英语表达方式。第3部分为其他服务，包含重点旅客服务、投诉处理、失物招领、应急处理及感谢、道歉与建议5个单元。每个单元包括导入、听说训练、阅读、拓展练习及自我评价五项学习任务。为了拓宽视野，提高专业知识阅读能力，在每个单元的拓展部分，分别介绍了中国、日本、法国和德国的现代轨道交通工具发展状况。

本书在编写过程中注重内容的系统性，学习内容涉及轨道交通客运服务的整个作业流程，模拟实际工作情境，充分体现高职教育实践性特征。教材编写体现了"工学结合、校企合作"的理念，行业专家、学者全程参与本教材的编审工作。本书可以作为高职高专相关专业的教学用书，也可以作为轨道交通行业职工或者相关从业人员自学及培训用书。

编写分工

本书由武汉铁路职业技术学院王媛媛、湖南高速铁路职业技术学院应婷婷担任主编，武汉铁路职业技术学院许媛、湖南高速铁路职业技术学院刘慧、湖南铁道职业技术学院黄辉担任副主编，中国铁路武汉局集团公司武汉动车段工程师王岳及湖南高速铁路职业技术学院陈泓宇、林春香、王薇也参与了编写工作，武汉铁路职业技术学院夏栋担任主审。本书具体编写分工如下:王媛媛编写第8、11、18单元,应婷婷编写第1、3单元及附录Ⅱ,刘慧编写第2单元,陈泓宇编写第4、5单元,林春香编写第6、7单元,许媛编写第9、10、12、13、17单元,王岳编写第15、16单元,王薇编写第14单元及附录Ⅰ,黄辉编写附录Ⅲ、Ⅳ、Ⅴ。全书由王媛媛统稿。

可与本教材配合使用的教学资源

本教材配套多媒体课件、对话音频及阅读译文,以供相关任课老师教学参考,需要者可通过加入职教铁路教学研讨群(教师专用QQ群:211163250)向人民交通出版社股份有限公司管理员编辑获取。

致谢

本书在编写过程中,得到了武汉铁路职业技术学院、湖南高速铁路职业技术学院、湖南铁道职业技术学院和中国铁路武汉局集团公司等单位有关领导和专家的指导和帮助,在此一并表示感谢。

由于编者水平有限,书中难免存在疏漏和错误之处,恳请各位专家、读者批评指正。最后,我们对所有为本书的完成和出版给予支持和帮助的相关人员表示最衷心的感谢。

编　者

2020年6月

目　　录

Part Ⅰ　Station Service(站厅服务)

Unit 1　Enquiry Office　2
Unit 2　Ticket Office　10
Unit 3　Entrance of the Station　19
Unit 4　Waiting Hall　28
Unit 5　On Board the Train　36
Unit 6　Exit of the Station　43
Unit 7　Station Broadcasting　51

Part Ⅱ　Train Service(列车服务)

Unit 8　Equipment Introduction　56
Unit 9　Welcoming Aboard　65
Unit 10　Service in the Carriage　73
Unit 11　Dining Car Service　85
Unit 12　Train Broadcasting　94
Unit 13　Getting Off the Train　103

Part Ⅲ　Other Services(其他服务)

Unit 14　Special Passenger Service　111
Unit 15　Complaints　119
Unit 16　Lost and Found　126
Unit 17　Emergency Response　133
Unit 18　Thanks, Apologies and Advice　141
Appendix　149
　Ⅰ.铁路客运服务词汇　149

Ⅱ. 餐饮词汇 ·· 151
Ⅲ. 火车站 ·· 154
Ⅳ. 旅游词汇 ·· 159
Ⅴ. 日常用语 ·· 168

参考文献 ·· 170

Part I

Station Service（站厅服务）

Unit 1

Enquiry Office

Section A: Starting Out

Look at the following signs of railway transportation and try to guess what they are.

Enquiry Office/Information Office　　Waiting Room　　Elevator
Luggage Storage Office　　Luggage Office　　Direction Arrow
Washing Room　　Maternal and Infant Waiting Room

1. _____

2. _____

3. _____

4. _____

Part I/Unit 1　Enquiry Office

5. _____

6. _____

7. _____

8. _____

 Section B: Listening and Speaking

SETTING: AT THE INFORMATION/ENQUIRY OFFICE A PASSENGER IS ASKING FOR INFORMATION. (P = PASSENGER, C = CLERK)

Conversation 1

Activity 1: Listen and answer.
1. Which train should I take for Shanghai at around 10:00?
2. Where is the TVM (Ticket Vending Machine)?

Activity 2: Listen again and fill in the blanks.
1. _____, can you tell me where the _____ is?
2. You can buy the ticket from the _____.

Activity 3: Work in pairs. Read the conversation at least twice, changing roles each time.

C: Good morning! Can I help you?
P: Which train should I take for Shanghai at around 10:00?
C: Let me check. You can take train G13.
P: Thank you! By the way, can you tell me where the ticket office is?
C: It's on the first floor. You can buy the ticket from the Ticket Vending Machine.
P: Great! Where is the TVM?
C: The TVM is on the right of the ticket office.
P: Thank you.
C: You are welcome.

Activity 4: Please make up your own dialogue with the given information.

A passenger will go to Guangzhou, but he doesn't know which train he should take. He is asking something about it in the Enquiry Office.

Conversation 2

Activity 1: Listen and answer.

1. Which platform does the train G121 depart from?
2. What can I do if I can't catch my train?

Activity 2: Listen again and fill in the blanks.

1. You can go to the _____ to _____ your ticket.
2. The _____ is on the first floor.

Activity 3: Work in pairs. Read the conversation at least twice, changing roles each time.

P: Excuse me. Is this the Enquiry Office?
C: Yes, it is. What can I do for you?
P: Which platform does the train G121 depart from?
C: It departs from Platform 2.
P: What can I do if I can't catch my train?
C: You can go to the ticket office to change your ticket. The Refund/Rebooking Window is on the first floor.
P: I get it. Thank you very much.
C: My pleasure.

Activity 4: Please make up your own dialogue based on the following situation.

A passenger will take G72 to Wuhan, but he doesn't know which platform the train departs from and he doesn't know where the washroom is, so he is asking a clerk about the information.

Conversation 3

Activity 1: Listen and answer.

1. What can I do if I lost my ticket?
2. What materials do I need to provide when I am handling the replacement procedure?

Activity 2: Listen again and fill in the blanks.

1. You can get the same _____ of _____ ticket as the _____ ticket.
2. You need to _____ your ID Card, the date of the _____ and the name of the _____ issuing the _____.

Activity 3: Work in pairs. Read the conversation at least twice, changing roles each time.

> P: Excuse me, is this the Enquiry Office?
> C: Yes, it is. What can I do for you?
> P: I lost my High-speed Railway ticket for Guangzhou. What can I do?
> C: Don't worry. You can buy a replacement ticket at the ticket office.
> P: A replacement ticket?
> C: Yes, you can get the same seat number of replacement ticket as the original booked ticket.
> P: Really? That's very good. Do I need to provide any materials in handling the replacement procedure?
> C: Yes, you need to provide your ID Card, the date of the original ticket and the name

of the ticket office issuing the booked ticket.
P:Is any service charge required?
C:Five yuan.
P:Thank you very much.
C:Not at all.

Activity 4:Please make up your own dialogue based on the following situation.

A passenger didn't catch G1306 to Shanghai. He is asking something about it at the Enquiry Office.

 Words and Phrases ◂◂◂

ticket office			售票处
Ticket Vending Machine(TVM)			自动售票机
Enquiry Office			问讯处
depart	[dɪˈpɑːt]	v.	离开;出发
refund	[ˈriːfʌnd]	v.	退还;偿还
replacement	[rɪˈpleɪsmənt]	n.	代替;补充
handle	[ˈhændl]	v.	处理
ID Card			身份证
platform	[ˈplætfɔːm]	n.	站台
change	[tʃeɪndʒ]	v.	改变;改签
original	[əˈrɪdʒənl]	adj.	原始的;最初的
procedure	[prəˈsiːdʒə(r)]	n.	程序;过程;步骤
issue	[ˈɪʃuː]	v.	发行;发布;发给

 Section C:Passage Reading

Enquiry Office is very closely linked with people's daily lives. In China, many public services are equipped with the information desks, for example, hospitals, railway stations, docks, airports, and so on. Almost in every railway station, especially in high-speed railway station, there are Enquiry Offices. The sign of the information office is a question mark, which you can find it easily. The information office offers services and help for the passengers. You can ask all kinds of information there. It brings great convenience for people to seek advice. The Enquiry Office is usually located next to the ticket office or in the center of the waiting hall.

Part I/Unit 1　Enquiry Office

 Words and Phrases ◂◂◂

information desk			问讯处
question mark			问号
convenience	[kənˈviːnɪəns]	n.	方便；便利
locate	[ləʊˈkeɪt]	v.	位于
waiting hall			候车室

I. Terms translation

1. question mark
2. Enquiry Office
3. waiting hall
4. be equipped with
5. link with
6. seek advice

II. Sentences translation

1. Enquiry Office is very closely linked with people's daily lives.
2. The information office offers services and help for the passengers.
3. The information office brings great convenience for people to seek advice.
4. The Enquiry Office is usually located next to the ticket office or in the center of the waiting hall.

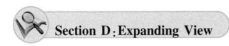

The Development of China's High-speed Railway

China's high-speed railway has made an astonishing progress during the last 10 years, undergoing a remarkable development from totally nothing to a widely expanding network, and learning other countries' techniques to getting ahead of them. Now there are 8 core high-speed railway lines across China, which is called "Four vertical and four horizontal" system. These 8 core lines link with other more than 30 stretches all over the vast land. By the end of 2017, the nation's high-speed railway system had attained a total length of over 25000km, which is 66.3% of the world's total of high-speed railways, much more than the sum of those set up in Japan, Germany, France, Spain and Italy, etc. And this has made China a world-leading nation in high-speed railway construction, with a highest running speed and a complete set of facilities.

According the nation's thirteenth five-year transportation plan, by the end of 2020, the nation's railway system is expected to reach 150000km. High-speed railways will reach 35000km, covering over 80% of cities with more than 1 million permanent residents. By that time, China will be covered with a mass transportation network of "eight vertical and eight horizontal" high-speed railway system.

Words and Phrases

astonishing	[əˈstɒnɪʃɪŋ]	adj.	使人吃惊的;惊人的
undergo	[ˌʌndəˈɡəʊ]	v.	经历;承受
remarkable	[rɪˈmɑːkəbl]	adj.	引人注目的;卓越的
get ahead of			胜过;超过
vertical	[ˈvɜːtɪkl]	adj.	纵长的;竖立的
horizontal	[ˌhɒrɪˈzɒntl]	adj.	水平的;地平线的
four vertical and four horizontal			四纵四横
stretch	[stretʃ]	v.	伸展;延伸
attain	[əˈteɪn]	v.	达到;获得
facility	[fəˈsɪləti]	n.	设备
permanent	[ˈpɜːmənənt]	adj.	永久的;永恒的
eight vertical and eight horizontal			八纵八横

Section E: Self-evaluation

Ⅰ. Words and phrases translation

1. 问讯处
2. 候车室
3. 行李托运处
4. 行李寄存处

5. 母婴候车室

6. 洗手间

7. 问号

8. 电梯

9. 方向箭头

10. 四纵四横

11. 补票

12. 订票

13. 退票

14. 改签

15. 身份证

16. 自动售票机

17. 胜过;超过

Ⅱ. Sentences translation

1. 乘坐哪些车可以去北京?

2. 能告诉我售票处在哪?

3. 售票处在候车室的东侧。

4. 你可以在自动售票机上购票。

5. 这趟列车在哪个站台发车?

6. 你可以去售票厅补票。

7. 补的票的座位号和原先的一样。

8. 办理补票手续我需要提供材料吗?

9. 在过去10年间,中国高铁事业的发展突飞猛进。

10. 中国是世界上高铁建设运营规模最大的国家,其运营速度和整体配套处于世界前列。

Unit 2

Ticket Office

Section A: Starting Out

Look at the following signs and pictures of railway transportation and try to guess what they are.

```
ticket office/booking office    ticket counter     ordinary train ticket
automatic ticket vending machine                   high-speed railway ticket
train timetable                 refund window      China Railway Service Center Website
```

1. _____

2. _____

3. _____

4. _____

Part I/Unit 2　Ticket Office

5. _____

6. _____

7. _____

8. _____

 Section B: Listening and Speaking

SETTING: AT THE TICKET/BOOKING OFFICE A PASSENGER IS ASKING FOR INFORMATION. (P = PASSENGER, C = CLERK)

Conversation 1

Activity 1: Listen and answer.

1. What kind of ticket will the foreign passenger want to buy?
2. How much is the hard berth ticket from Shenzhen to Beijing?

Activity 2: Listen again and fill in the blanks.

1. I want a _____ from Shenzhen to Beijing for tomorrow.
2. The hard berth ticket is 434.5 yuan. Will you show _____, please?

Activity 3: Work in pairs. Read the conversation at least twice, changing roles each time.

C: Good morning! Can I help you?
P: Hello! I want a hard berth ticket from Shenzhen to Beijing for tomorrow.

C: Sorry. There are only standing tickets left.

P: Could you please help to check if there is any hard berth ticket on Monday?

C: OK, wait a moment, please. Yes, we have hard berth tickets on Monday.

P: A hard berth ticket for Monday. Thank you. What's the fare, please?

C: The hard berth ticket is 434.5 yuan. Will you show me your passport please.

P: Oh, here you are. My passport and 450 yuan.

C: Here is your ticket, your change and your passport. Please check it.

P: Oh, Thank you.

C: You are welcome.

Activity 4: Please make up your own dialogue with the given information.

A foreign passenger will go to Wuhan by high-speed train, but he doesn't know which train to take. He is asking something about it at the ticket office.

Conversation 2

Activity 1: Listen and answer.

1. What kind of ticket will the passenger want to buy?

2. What is the child ticket standard, according to *China Railway Passenger Transport Rules and Regulations*?

Activity 2: Listen again and fill in the blanks.

1. I'd like to buy three _____ tickets to Shenzhen.

2. Each adult can bring along one child with height _____ for free.

Activity 3: Work in pairs. Read the conversation at least twice, changing roles each time.

C: Hello, can I help you?

P: Yes, I'd like to buy three high-speed train tickets to Shenzhen. One adult ticket, and two children tickets.

C: What's the height of your children?

P: One is 1.4m tall and the other is less than 1m.

C: Well, according to *China Railway Passenger Transport Rules and Regulations*, each adult can bring along one child with height less than 1.2m for free. Half price for more than one child or the ones with height from 1.2m to 1.5m. So, you may just buy one child ticket for the child over 1.4m. And the child less than 1.0m can share the ticket with you.

P:Oh, That's a good idea. I'll take one full fare ticket and one child ticket.
C:Thanks. Here you are.
P:Thank you very much.
C:My pleasure.

Activity 4: Please make up your own dialogue based on the following situation.

A passenger will bring two children to Beijing. One child is over 1.2m, and the other is over 1.4m. He is asking the clerk about the information.

Conversation 3

Activity 1: Listen and answer.

1. What should you pay if you want to refund your ticket?
2. What materials do I need to provide when I am handling the refunding procedure?

Activity 2: Listen again and fill in the blanks.

1. And you still need to show me your _____.
2. It's 20% of the ticket fare if the refunding is completed _____.

Activity 3: Work in pairs. Read the conversation at least twice, changing roles each time.

P:Excuse me, can you do me a favor?
C:Yes, of course. What can I do for you?
P:I bought a high-speed train ticket to Guangzhou yesterday. Can I get a refund for it?
C:Don't worry. Let me look at your ticket. Oh, there are 12h before your train's departure time and you can get the refund. But according to the regulations, you have to pay a refund service surcharge.
P:OK, how much is the fee?
C:It's 20% of the ticket fare if the refunding is completed within 24h before departure.
P:OK.
C:And you still need to show me your valid ID Card.
P:Here you are.
C:Thank you. Here is the refund.
P:Thank you very much.
C:You are welcome.

Activity 4:Please make up your own dialogue based on the following situation.

A passenger can't take the high-speed train to Shanghai the day after tomorrow, so he is asking something about refunding the ticket in the ticket office.

(The refunding surcharges are as follows: It's 5% of the ticket fare for refunds completed over 48h before departure, 10% of the ticket fare for refunds completed between 24-48h before departure, and 20% of the ticket fare for refunds completed within 24h before departure.)

Words and Phrases ◂◂◂

hard berth ticket			硬卧票
standing ticket			站票
fare	[feə(r)]	n.	费;票价
rule	[ruːl]	n.	规则;规定
regulation	[ˌreɡjuˈleɪʃn]	n.	规章;规则
adult ticket			成人票
child ticket			儿童票
complete	[kəmˈpliːt]	v.	完成;结束
departure	[dɪˈpɑːtʃə(r)]	n.	离开;离去
surcharge	[ˈsɜːtʃɑːdʒ]	n.	附加费;额外费用
valid	[ˈvælɪd]	adj.	有效的

Section C:Passage Reading

How to Buy China Train Tickets

Tips for passengers:

Train tickets of China can be bought in the following 4 ways:

1. Book tickets from online agencies like Travel China Guide.

2. Buy tickets at railway stations or ticket outlets.

3. Book tickets from http://www.12306.cn/, the official website of China Railway Service Center.

4. Reserve tickets via 95105105, the official hotline.

The valid certificates required for buying the tickets include:

Second-generation ID Cards; passport for foreign passengers; or Mainland Travel Permits for Hong Kong, Macao and Taiwan passengers.

Ticketing officially starts 30 days before departure.

Pre-sale time for China railway tickets is now 30 days before departure on the official website and via hotline of the China Railway Corporation, and 28 days in advance at railway stations and ticket outlets.

Useful Tips:

The pre-sale period may be adjusted during the rush holidays or festivals. To play it safe you should book through an agency as early as possible.

If you are unable to leave on schedule, you can refund or change the ticket at any railway station. If you lost a ticket, you can reclaim the booked seat or sleeper with your valid ID certificate.

The ticket price does not include insurance and you need to buy travel insurance separately.

Children who stand between 3.9 feet (1.2m) and 4.9 feet (1.5m) tall need to buy children's tickets while those under 3.9 feet (1.2m) ride for free. Please note that children are accompanied by adults as a rule.

Words and Phrases

ticket outlets			售票点
corporation	[kɔːpəˈreɪʃn]	n.	公司;法人
Mainland Travel Permit		n.	来往内地通行证
pre-sale period			预售期
via	[ˈvaɪə]	prep.	通过;经由
adjust	[əˈdʒʌst]	v.	调整;适应
rush holidays			旅行高峰期
agency	[ˈeɪdʒənsɪ]	n.	代理机构;中介
on schedule			按时;按照预定时间
reclaim	[rɪˈkleɪm]	v.	收回;取回
certificate	[səˈtɪfɪkeɪt]	n.	证书;执照
insurance	[ɪnˈʃʊərəns]	n.	保险;保险费
separately	[ˈseprətlɪ]	adv.	分别地;单独地
be accompanied by			伴随;陪伴;陪同

 Exercises

Ⅰ. Terms translation

1. ticket outlets
2. Mainland Travel Permit for Hong Kong, Macao and Taiwan passengers
3. the pre-sale period
4. reclaim the booked seat
5. valid ID certificate
6. buy travel insurance

II. Sentences translation

1. Ticketing officially starts 30 days before departure.
2. The pre-sale period may be adjusted during the rush holidays or festivals.
3. If you lost a ticket, you can reclaim the booked seat/sleeper with your valid ID certificate.
4. The ticket price does not include insurance and you need to buy travel insurance separately.

 Section D: Expanding View

Fuxing, China's Newest Model of the Country's High-speed Bullet Trains

Fuxing, China's newest model of the country's high-speed bullet trains, made its debut on the Beijing—Shanghai high-speed railway line in June, 2017.

Fuxing, which means rejuvenation, is the first bullet train designed and manufactured entirely by Chinese engineers. With a top speed of 400km/h, its launch heralds a new era for the Chinese high-speed railway and lays the foundation for China to export its high-speed railway technologies.

A Fuxing bullet train left Beijing South Railway Station to Shanghai along the Beijing—Shanghai high-speed route on Sept. 21st, 2017. China increased the maximum speed of bullet trains on the Beijing—Shanghai route to 350km/h.

With the new-generation high-speed bullet trains Fuxing put into service for key cities in September 2017, travelling time from Tianjin Railway Station to Beijing South Railway Station had been cut from 30min to under 25min.

Fully designed and manufactured in China, the Fuxing trains (can hit a top speed of 400km/h), run at 350km/h, faster than Japan's famous Shinkansen trains (with an operating speed of 300km/h) and France's TGVs trains (with an operating speed of 320km/h).

The Fuxing trains are a substantial upgrade on the previous Hexie (Harmony) bullet trains. The Fuxing trains are more spacious and energy-efficient, with longer service life and better reliability.

Words and Phrases

bullet trains			子弹头列车
make its debut			首次亮相
rejuvenation	[rɪˌdʒuːvəˈneɪʃn]	n.	恢复活力
entirely	[ɪnˈtaɪəli]	adv.	完全地;彻底地
launch	[lɔːntʃ]	v.	发起;投入
herald	[ˈherəld]	v.	通报;预示……的来临
era	[ˈɪərə]	n.	时代;年代
lay the foundation			奠定基础
export	[ˈekspɔːt]	v.	输出;出口
increase	[ɪnˈkriːs]	v.	增加;加大
maximum	[ˈmæksɪməm]	adj.	最高的;最多的
hit a top speed			最高速度
operating speed			运营速度
substantial	[səbˈstænʃl]	adj.	大量的;实质的;内容充实的
upgrade	[ʌpˈɡreɪd]	n.	升级
previous	[ˈpriːviəs]	adj.	以前的;早先的
spacious	[ˈspeɪʃəs]	adj.	宽敞的;广阔的
energy-efficient		adj.	节能的;高能效的
service life			使用寿命
reliability	[rɪˌlaɪəˈbɪləti]	n.	可靠性

Section E: Self-evaluation

I. Words and phrases translation

1. 售票处
2. 自动售票机
3. 高铁车票
4. 中国铁路客户服务中心网站
5. 卧铺票
6. 硬卧票
7. 站票
8. 中国铁路旅客运输管理规则
9. 儿童票
10. 退票
11. 退票手续费
12. 有效身份证件

13. 补办车票

14. 最高时速

15. 二代身份证

16. 运营速度

17. 购买旅行保险

Ⅱ. Sentences translation

1. 北京到上海的高铁票价格是多少?

2. 我要买两张明天从北京到深圳的硬卧票。

3. 对不起,现在只有站票了。

4. 每位成人可以免费携带一名身高 1.2m 以下的儿童。

5. 离开车时间不足 24 小时办理退票的,按票价 20% 计算退票费。

6. "复兴号"动车组列车的设计制造全部由中国完成。

7. "复兴号"是第一辆由中国工程师独立设计制造的高铁。

8. 今年 9 月,高速列车"复兴号"在中国主要城市投入使用。

9. "复兴号"最高速度可以达到 400km/h。

Part I/Unit 3　Entrance of the Station

Unit 3

Entrance of the Station

 Section A : Starting Out

Look at the following signs and pictures of railway transportation and try to guess what they are.

```
Boarding Gate           Contraband          Security Check
Entrance                Platform
Ticket Checking Machine                     Electronic Display
Automatic Face-recognition System
```

1. _____　　　2. _____

3. _____　　　4. _____

枪支 FIREARMS　　弹药 AMMUNITION　　警械 POLICEWEAPONS

易燃易爆 FLAMMABLE EXPLOSIVES　　腐蚀品 CORROSIVES　　钝器 BLUNTMATERIAL

管制刀具 CONTROLED KNIFE　　放射物品 RADIOACTIVE　　氧化剂 OXIDISING

利器 SHARPMATERIAL　　强磁物品 MAGNETIZED　　毒害品 POISONS

5. _____

6. _____

7. _____

8. _____

Part I/Unit 3 Entrance of the Station

Section B: Listening and Speaking

Conversation 1

SETTING: A PASSENGER IS ASKING FOR INFORMATION ABOUT BOARDING GATE AND PLATFORM. (P = PASSENGER, C = CLERK)

Activity 1: Listen and answer.
1. Where can the passenger get on the train?
2. Where is the boarding gate?

Activity 2: Listen again and fill in the blanks.
1. There is a big _____ on the entrance.
2. It is showing _____ , _____ and _____ .

Activity 3: Work in pairs. Read the conversation at least twice, changing roles each time.

C: Good afternoon. What could I do for you?
P: Good afternoon. I want to take the train to Wuhan. Where can I get on the train?
C: Show me your ticket, please.
P: Here you are.
C: Your boarding gate is No. 6. It departs from platform 1. Here is a big electronic screen on the entrance. It is showing Train No. , boarding gates and platforms. You can find your boarding gate and platform on the screen.
P: I see. Thank you. Where is the boarding gate?
C: The boarding gate is on the second floor.
P: Thank you very much.
C: You are welcome.

Activity 4: Please make up your own dialogue based on the following situation.

A passenger doesn't know where to check his ticket. He is asking something about the boarding gate at the entrance of station. Suppose you are a clerk, you will help him to find his boarding gate.

铁路客运服务英语

Conversation 2

SETTING: A PASSENGER IS ASKING FOR INFORMATION ABOUT AUTOMATIC FACE-RECOGNITION SYSTEM.

Activity 1: Listen and answer.

1. What kind of system the station has adopted?
2. How to use the Automatic Face-recognition System?

Activity 2: Listen again and fill in the blanks.

1. This is _____.
2. Place your ticket on top of your _____ and wait for the machine to _____ the ticket' QR Code (Quick Response Code).

Activity 3: Work in pairs. Read the conversation at least twice, changing roles each time.

P: Excuse me, what is this?

C: This is Automatic Face-recognition System. Our station has adopted an Automatic Face-recognition System to help passengers get into the station quickly.

P: Oh, sounds great! How can I use it?

C: Place your ticket on top of your ID Card and wait for the machine to scan the ticket' QR Code, then look at the camera. After the camera records your face and the system verifies the ID information, you are allowed to enter the station.

P: OK. Let me try. Like this?

C: Yes, that's right.

P: It's convenient and fast. Thank you.

C: You are welcome.

Activity 4: Please make up your own dialogue based on the following situation.

A passenger wants to get through Automatic Face-recognition System, but he doesn't know how to use it. He is asking something about Automatic Face-recognition System. Suppose you are a clerk, you will tell him how to use it.

Conversation 3

SETTING: A PASSENGER IS GOING THROUGH SECURITY CHECK.

Activity 1: Listen and answer.

1. What's wrong with the passenger's security check?
2. What did the clerk ask him to do?

Activity 2: Listen again and fill in the blanks.

1. Everyone has to accept the _____ no matter what's in the package.
2. Please put your bag on _____ to get screened by _____ .

Activity 3: Work in pairs. Read the conversation at least twice, changing roles each time.

C: Excuse me, sir. Security check, please.

P: I just have some books in my bag.

C: Everyone has to accept the security check. This is the rule.

P: OK, I'll follow it.

C: Please put your bag on the conveyer belt to get screened by X-ray equipment.

P: OK.

C: Oh, sir. Is there a knife in your bag?

P: Yeah. What's up? I would like to take this souvenir as a gift to a friend.

C: I'm sorry to tell you that it is a prohibited item. The knife is not permitted to be taken on the train.

P: Sorry, I didn't know that.

C: We have to detain this knife for the time being. You must come here to get it back in one month. Or you can give it up.

P: OK, I'll give it up.

C: Thank you for your cooperation.

Activity 4: Please make up your own dialogue based on the fallowing situation.

A passenger's suitcase is been screened by X-ray equipment at the security check. A clerk detects a bottle of hairspray in her bag. Suppose you are the clerk. How do you deal with it?

Words and Phrases

Automatic Face-recognition System			自动人脸识别系统
QR Code(Quick Response Code)			二维码
security check			安检
conveyer belt			传送带
souvenir	[ˌsuːvəˈnɪə(r)]		纪念品
permit	[pəˈmɪt]	v.	许可;允许
adopt	[əˈdɒpt]	v.	采用
verify	[ˈverɪfaɪ]	v.	证实
X-ray equipment			X射线设备
screen	[skriːn]	v.	扫描
prohibited item			违禁品
detain	[dɪˈteɪn]	v.	扣留

Section C: Passage Reading

Automatic Face-recognition System

The Beijing west Railway Station has adopted an Automatic Face-recognition System to help passengers get into the station more quickly as the Spring Festival Travel Rush is coming. The new system is quicker and more convenient.

The passengers can get through the checkpoints within 10s by placing their tickets on top of their Identification Cards and waiting for the machine to scan the tickets' QR Code. After the camera records their faces and the system verifies the ID information, passengers are allowed to enter the station.

However, not all passengers could check in through the Face-identification System, including those who buy student tickets or other kinds of discounted tickets and foreigners who use their passports.

Railway station may expand Automatic Face-recognition System's usage if everything goes well.

Part I/Unit 3 Entrance of the Station

 Words and Phrases

Spring Festival Travel Rush			春运高峰
Identification Card			身份证
discounted ticket			打折票
checkpoint	['tʃekpɔɪnt]	n.	安检/检查站
get through			通过
student ticket			学生票
passport	['pɑːspɔːt]	n.	护照

 # Exercises

I. Terms translation

1. Automatic Face-recognition System
2. QR Code
3. discounted ticket
4. passport

II. Sentences translation

1. The Beijing West Railway Station has adopted an Automatic Face-recognition System.
2. The new system is quicker and more convenient.
3. Place their tickets on top of their Identification Cards and wait for the machine to scan the tickets' QR Code.
4. The camera records their faces and the system verifies the ID information.

 Section D: Passage Reading

The Development of China's High-speed Railway

China planed to spend 732 billion yuan ($112.7 billion) on railway projects in 2018. Some 4000km of new tracks were planned to be put into operation in the coming year, and 3500km would be high-speed railway tracks, Lu Dongfu, general manager of China Railway Corp., the nation's railway operator, said during the company's annual meeting.

"Between 2013 and 2017, China had spent 3.9 trillion yuan on railway projects, making it a record period for intensive, mass investment on the railway system," he said. During those years, 29400km of new tracks have been built, and more than half—15700km—were for high-speed trains.

In 2017, China spent 801 billion yuan on railways and put 3038km of new tracks into operation. By the end of 2017, the nation's railway system reached a total length of 127000km, including 25000km of high-speed tracks, which was 66.3% of the world's total high-speed railways.

Words and Phrases

track	[træk]	n.	轨道;线路
China Railway Corp.			中国铁路总公司
trillion	[ˈtrɪljən]	n.	万亿
investment	[ɪnˈvestmənt]	n.	投资
put into operation			投入运营
billion	[ˈbɪljən]	n.	十亿
intensive	[ɪnˈtensɪv]	adj.	加强的
total length			总长

Section E: Self-evaluation

Ⅰ. Words and phrases translation

1. 检票口
2. 进站口
3. 站台
4. 自动售票机
5. 人脸识别系统
6. 安检
7. 二维码
8. 身份证
9. X 射线设备
10. 违禁品
11. 护照
12. 新线
13. 投入运营
14. 中国铁路总公司
15. 总长

Ⅱ. Sentences translation

1. 您可以在屏幕上找到您的车次和检票口。
2. 您的检票口是 6 号检票口，您在 1 号站台上车。
3. 这是自动人脸识别系统。

4. 将车票放在身份证上面,并让机器扫描车票上的二维码。

5. 看着摄像头。

6. 每个人都要接受安检。

7. 请把你的包放在传送带上。

8. 很抱歉告诉你,这是违禁品。

9. 小刀不允许带上高铁。

10. 我们得暂时扣留这把小刀。

11. 谢谢合作。

12. 新的系统更快捷,更方便。

13. 并不是所有的乘客都可以通过自动人脸识别系统检票。

14. 截至2017年底,全国铁路营业里程达12.7万 km,其中高铁2.5万 km,占世界高铁总里程的66.3%。

Unit 4

Waiting Hall

Section A: Starting Out

Look at the following signs of railway transportation and try to guess what they are.

Maternal and Infant Waiting Room	Waiting Room	Ticket Check
Teahouse	Shopping Mall	Exit
Washing Room	Soft Seat Waiting Room	

1. _____

2. _____

3. _____

4. _____

Part I/Unit 4 Waiting Hall

5. _____

6. _____

7. _____

8. _____

 Section B: Listening and Speaking

SETTING: IN THE WAITING HALL, A PASSENGER IS ASKING FOR INFORMATION.
(P = PASSENGER, C = CLERK)

Conversation 1

Activity 1: Listen and answer.
1. Where can I wait for Train T21 to Shanghai?
2. Should I pay for it if I go to the VIP room?

Activity 2: Listen again and fill in the blanks.
1. I'm taking T21 to Shanghai, will you please tell me where I can _____?
2. You can also _____ in the VIP room.

Activity 3: Work in pairs. Read the conversation at least twice, changing roles each time.

C: Good morning! Ticket, please.
P: Good morning! I'm taking T21 to Shanghai, will you please tell me where I can wait for the train?
C: You can wait for the train in the No. 3 waiting room on the second floor, or you can also have a rest in the VIP room.
P: Should I pay for it if I go to the VIP room?
C: No, since you have bought a cushioned ticket, you can have a good rest there free of charge.
P: Thank you.
C: You're welcome.

Activity 4: Please make up your own dialogue with the given information.

A passenger is in the waiting room and he feels very boring, so he wants to go somewhere else. A clerk reminds him to check in 40min later.

Conversation 2

Activity 1: Listen and answer.
1. What time does the train leave?
2. What time is it now?

Activity 2: Listen again and fill in the blanks.
1. Your train is _____ at 20:30.
2. _____ will be announced over the loudspeaker.

Activity 3: Work in pairs. Read the conversation at least twice, changing roles each time.

C: What can I do for you?
P: Yes. Is this the waiting hall for my train?
C: Yes, it is. Please show me your ticket.
P: OK. Here it is.
C: Thank you. Please sit down and wait. Your train is due to leave at 20:30. You have 50 minutes to spare. Boarding time will be announced over the loudspeaker.
P: I see. Thank you.
C: My pleasure.

Activity 4: Please make up your own dialogue based on the following situation.

A passenger is waiting for the train. Carrying several bags along with him, he asks a clerk about how to deposit them at the information desk.

Conversation 3

Activity 1: Listen and answer.

1. Where is the VIP room?
2. Where can I get the newspapers or magazines?

Activity 2: Listen again and fill in the blanks.

1. I'm looking for the _____. Can you tell me where it is?
2. You could read some newspapers and magazines, or watch some _____ here before your train _____.

Activity 3: Work in pairs. Read the conversation at least twice, changing roles each time.

C: Excuse me, what can I do for you?
P: I'm looking for the VIP waiting room. Can you tell me where it is?
C: It's on the second floor. Come along with me, please.
P: Thank you.
C: Here it is. Please show me your ticket and VIP Card.
P: Here you are.
C: OK. Please sit down and have a rest. You could read some newspapers and magazines, or watch some TV programs here before your train is leaving.
P: All right. By the way, where can I get the newspapers or magazines?
C: You can get them from the table in the Hall.
P: I see. Thank you.
C: You're welcome.

Activity 4: Please make up your own dialogue based on the fallowing situation.

Suppose you are in the waiting room, a man comes to you and begs for your help. He wants you to take care of his luggage for a while.

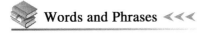
Words and Phrases

waiting room   候车室

cushioned ticket			软席票
board	[bɔːd]	v.	上（船、飞机等）
due to			由于；因为
VIP Card			贵宾卡
VIP waiting room			贵宾室
loudspeaker	[laʊdˈspiːkə]	n.	扬声器；喇叭
boarding time			上车时间
free of charge			免费
luggage	[ˈlʌɡɪdʒ]	n.	行李

Section C: Passage Reading

The waiting room, no matter what the size, is equipped with a certain amount of infrastructures, such as toilets, boiled water, stores, public telephone service and other necessary facilities. Generally there is central heating (winter) or cooling (summer) opening in it. Some rooms in good condition provide video security equipment. Waiting rooms are equipped with a certain number of seats for passengers waiting for their trains and some special waiting areas for special needs, such as maternal and infant lounges and soldiers' waiting rooms. Addition to the hardware, software services can also basically meet the needs of the waiting passengers. Regular cleaning remains a good environment for passengers, and magazine sale service is also offered to help waiting passengers to kill time.

Words and Phrases

infrastructure	[ˈɪnfrəstrʌktʃə]	n.	基础设施
kill time			打发时间
maternal	[məˈtɜːnl]	adj.	母亲的
infant	[ˈɪnfənt]	adj.	幼儿的；婴儿的
facility	[fəˈsɪlɪti]	n.	设施
waiting hall			候车室
video security equipment			监控设备

Exercises

Ⅰ. Terms translation

1. boiled water
2. central heating
3. video security equipment

4. software service

5. kill time

II. Sentences translation

1. Some rooms in good condition provide video security equipment.

2. Regular cleaning remains a good environment for passengers.

3. Generally there is central heating (winter) or cooling (summer) opening in it.

4. Addition to the hardware, software services can also basically meet the needs of the waiting passengers.

Section D: Expanding View

The Introduction of Japan's High-speed Railway

Japan was the first country to build dedicated railway lines for high-speed travel. The Tokaido Shinkansen(东海道新干线) was put into commercial service on Oct. 1st, 1964. On its run between Tokyo and Osaka, the train reached the speed of 210km/h. The one-way journey used to take 6h and 30min, but the new train shortened that to 3h.

In Japan, high-speed railway was called Shinkansen(新干线), which is colloquially known in English as the bullet train. It is a network of high-speed railway lines in Japan operated by 5 Japan Railway Group companies, and plays an important role in daily travelling of Japanese people.

Up to April, 2017, Japan had owned a high-speed railway network of 3021km. In order to highlight the importance of high-speed railway in land transportation network, Japan planed to build more high-speed railways. The main high-speed railways in Japan are as followings: Tokaido Shinkansen(东海道新干线), covers a distance of 515.4km; Sanyo Shinkansen(山阳新干线),

553.7km；Tohoku Shinkansen（东北新干线）,729.2km；Joetsu Shinkansen（上越新干线），369.5km；Hokuriku Shinkansen（北陆新干线），117.4km.

Words and Phrases

Shinkansen	[ˈʃiːnkɑːnˌsen]	n.	新干线
put into commercial service			投入运营
shorten	[ˈʃɔːtn]	v.	缩短
dedicated	[ˈdedɪkeɪtɪd]	adj.	专有的
one-way journey			单程旅行
highlight	[ˈhaɪˌlaɪt]	v.	凸显；强调

Section E: Self-evaluation

Ⅰ. Words and phrases translation.

1. 茶座
2. 候车室
3. 贵宾室
4. 软席候车室
5. 洗手间
6. 购物中心
7. 投入运营
8. 基础设施
9. 打发时间
10. 缩短
11. 监控设备
12. 子弹头列车
13. 单程旅行
14. 新干线
15. 上车时间
16. 免费

Ⅱ. Sentences translation

1. 在贵宾室休息需要付费吗？
2. 因为您购买了软座票，您可以在贵宾室免费休息。
3. 能告诉我贵宾室在哪吗？
4. 广播会通知您上车时间。

5. 您乘坐的车将在 20:30 开出,您还需要等 50 分钟。
6. 我在哪儿可以拿到报纸和杂志?
7. 请出示您的车票和贵宾卡。
8. 日本是世界上第一个建成专有高速铁路线路的国家。
9. 新干线在日本人民的日常出行中发挥着重要的作用。

Unit 5

On Board the Train

Section A: Starting Out

Look at the following signs of railway transportation and try to guess what they are.

```
Clinic              Announcer Room      Ticket Check
Elevator            No Smoking          Security Check
Direction Arrow     Police
```

1. _____

2. _____

3. _____

4. _____

Part I/Unit 5 On Board the Train

5. _____

6. _____

7. _____

8. _____

 Section B: Listening and Speaking

SETTING: A CONDUCTOR/CONDUCTRESS IS STANDING AT THE CAR GATE TO CHECK THE PASSENGERS' TICKETS AND WELCOME THE PASSENGERS ABOARD. (P = PASSENGER, C = CONDUCTOR/CONDUCTRESS)

Conversation 1

Activity 1: Listen and answer.

1. What has happened to the passenger?
2. Where can the passenger catch the train?

Activity 2: Listen again and fill in the blanks.

1. I was _____ that I went to the wrong platform.
2. Z18 is standing on platform 3, just _____ of this platform.

Activity 3: Work in pairs. Read the conversation at least twice, changing roles each time.

C: Good morning, Sir. Ticket, please.
P: OK. Here you are.
C: Sorry, this is K186 to Guangzhou. You're catching Z18 to Shanghai.

P:Ah, I was so hurried that I went to the wrong platform. Will you please tell me where I can catch Z18?

C:Don't worry. Z18 is standing on platform 3, just on the other side of this platform. You have enough time to catch the train.

P:Thank you very much.

C:You're welcome.

Activity 4:Please make up your own dialogue with the given information.

A passenger is waiting for his turn to board the train, but the conductor tells him that the date on his ticket is tomorrow not today.

Conversation 2

Activity 1:Listen and answer.

1. Are you catching the K186?
2. What is boarding time for K186?

Activity 2:Listen again and fill in the blanks.

1. Sorry, you're catching K186, _____?
2. Please take your ticket back and go back to _____.

Activity 3:Work in pairs. Read the conversation at least twice, changing roles each time.

C:Show me your ticket, please.

P:Here it is.

C:Thank you. (After checking.) Sorry, you're catching K186, aren't you?

P:Yes, K186 to Zhengzhou.

C:But this is K221 to Guangzhou. Please take your ticket back and go back to the Waiting Hall. Boarding time for you is 11:26 a.m.

P:Thank you.

Activity 4:Please make up your own dialogue based on the following situation.

A passenger is going to the wrong boarding gate. He is asking a station clerk for help. Suppose you are the station clerk, you will offer some advice to the passenger.

Conversation 3

Activity 1:Listen and answer.

1. What is the passenger's car number?
2. How to get to the car No.16?

Activity 2:Listen again and fill in the blanks.

1. You can't _____. Here is your ticket back.
2. Thank you very much. Just continue in _____ ,right?

Activity 3:Work in pairs. Read the conversation at least twice, changing roles each time.

C:Good afternoon, Madam, would you please show me your ticket?

P:Sure. Here you are.

C:Thank you! Sorry, this is Car No.6, but your car is NO.16. Just follow the numbered signs and continue in this direction until you see a sign NO.16. You can't miss it. Here is your ticket back.

P:Oh, let me see, yes, NO.16. Thank you very much. Just continue in this direction, right?

C:Yes. Have a good trip!

P:Thank you.

C:You are welcome.

Activity 4:Please make up your own dialogue based on the following situation.

A passenger goes to the wrong car. Suppose you are the conductor, please help him to find the correct car.

Words and Phrases

platform	[ˈplætfɔːm]	n.	站台
sign	[saɪn]	n.	标志
car	[kɑː]	n.	车厢
stand	[stænd]	v.	停靠

Section C: Passage Reading

It's obvious that there is an ID certificates brush area in the upper part of the automatic ticket machine. As long as you put the second-generation ID Card on it, the automatic ticket machine will identify whether you bought effective high-speed railway tickets. If it is effective, you will be automatically released. The whole process is finished in about one second. Currently many high-speed railway routes support 4 real-name certificates, namely the resident ID Cards, Mainland Travel Permits for Hong Kong, Macao and Taiwan Residents, and passports. If you don't use second-generation ID Card but other certificates when you buy tickets on the Internet, you still need to go to the station ticket office or ticket agency for paper tickets in advance.

Words and Phrases

brush	[brʌʃ]	v.	刷
ID certificates brush area			身份证件识别区
effective	[ɪˈfektɪv]	adj.	有效的
in advance			提前；预先
identify	[aɪˈdentɪfaɪ]	v.	识别
automatic ticket machine			自动检票机
release	[rɪˈliːs]	v.	释放
ticket window			售票窗口

Exercises

I. Terms translation

1. ID certificates brush area
2. automatic ticket machine
3. high-speed railway tickets
4. in advance
5. ticket window

II. Sentences translation

1. If it is effective, you will be automatically released.
2. The whole process is finished in about one second.
3. It's obvious that there is an ID certificates brush area in the upper part of the automatic ticket machine.
4. As long as you put the second-generation ID Card on it, the automatic ticket machine will identify whether you bought effective high-speed train tickets.

Section D: Expanding View

The Introduction of French high-speed Railway

High-speed railway in France is called TGV (Train à Grande Vitesse). The idea of the TGV was first proposed in the 1960s, after Japan had begun construction of the Shinkansen (also known as the "bullet train") in 1959.

TGV was operated by SNCF (Société Nationale des Chemins de Francais), the national railway operator. It was developed in the 1970s by GEC-Alsthom and the SNCF. The first French high-speed railway line opened in 1981, between Paris's and Lyon's suburbs. It was the only high-speed railway line in Europe at that time.

On April 3rd, 2007, a TGV test train set a speed record of 574.8km/h, which is much faster than wheeled train. Up to July, 2017, France had owned a high-speed railway network of approximately 2647km, with 4 additional lines under construction. This network radiates from Paris, and plays an important role in French railway transportation.

 Words and Phrases

propose	[prəˈpəʊz]	v.	ˈ提出;提议
GEC-Alsthom			阿尔斯通公司
approximately	[əˈprɒksɪmɪtlɪ]	adv.	近似地;大约
additional	[əˈdɪʃənl]	adj.	另外的;额外的
operate	[ˈɒpəreɪt]	v.	经营
wheeled train			轮式列车
under construction			(正在)修建中

radiate　　　　　　　　　['reɪdɪeɪt]　　　　　v.　　呈辐射状发出；从中心发散

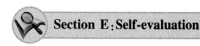

Ⅰ. Words and phrases translation

1. 小件托运
2. 广播室
3. 公安值班室
4. 请勿吸烟
5. 投入运营
6. 自动检票机
7. 身份证件识别区
8. （正在）修建中
9. 辐射
10. 大约
11. 预先；提前
12. 售票窗口
13. 额外的
14. 提出；提议

Ⅱ. Sentences translation

1. 能否告诉我在哪搭乘 Z18 次列车？
2. Z18 次列车停靠在 3 号站台，就在这个站台对面。
3. 你的上车时间是 11:26。
4. 请拿回你的车票，回候车室休息。
5. 如果是有效的，你就能被放行。
6. 很明显，在自动检票机顶端有身份证件识别区。
7. 只要你将身份证放入识别区，自动检票机就能识别你购买的高铁票是否有效。
8. 法国第一条高速铁路于 1981 年开通，往返巴黎和里昂的郊区。
9. TGV 列车打破了轮式火车的速度记录，2007 年 4 月 3 日创下了 574.8km/h 的速度记录。

Unit 6

Exit of the Station

 Section A: Starting Out

Look at the following signs at station exits and try to guess what they are.

| Subway | Exit | Bus | Ticket Office |
| Luggage Claim | Taxi | Transfer | Underground Car Park |

1. _____

2. _____

3. _____

4. _____

5. _____

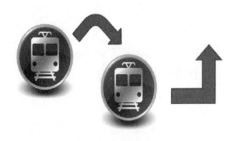

6. _____

7. _____

8. _____

Section B: Listening and Speaking

SETTING: AT THE STATION EXIT SOME PASSENGERS ARE GOING OUT, AND THE CLERK IS CHECKING THEIR TICKETS. (P = PASSENGER, C = CLERK)

Conversation 1

Activity 1: Listen and answer.

1. How long did the train delay?
2. How much is the ticket for Train G118 to Changsha?

Activity 2: Listen again and fill in the blanks.

1. You don't need to pay _____ for the new ticket.
2. Show the _____ to the ticket clerk and they will give you a new ticket after you _____ .

Activity 3: Work in pairs. Read the conversation at least twice, changing roles each time.

C: Good afternoon! Your ticket, please!
P: Here you are.
C: Thank you. (After checking) Have your ticket back, please.
P: Thank you! By the way, this train is supposed to get here 2h ago. The delay has made me missed Train G118 to Changsha.
C: Don't worry. You can change the ticket at the ticket office.
P: Yes. But this ticket cost me 206 yuan.
C: You don't need to pay a full fare for the new ticket. Show the original one to the ticket clerk and they will give you a new ticket after you balance the price difference.
P: That's great. Thank you so much.
C: You are welcome.

Activity 4: Please make up your own dialogue with the given information.

You have bought a joint ticket, but you can't find the transfer access when you get off at Hengyangdong Station.

Conversation 2

Activity 1: Listen and answer.

1. Why does the passenger feel anxious?
2. Does the passenger know how to use DiDi App?

Activity 2: Listen again and fill in the blanks.

1. Have you got the address you are _____?
2. Maybe you can _____, which is just like Uber in your country.

Activity 3: Work in pairs. Read the conversation at least twice, changing roles each time.

C: Good evening. May I have your ticket?
P: Sure! Here it is.
C: Thank you. Well, do you need any help? It seems that you are feeling anxious.
P: Yes. You know this is my first time here. My friend said he would be here to meet me, but he couldn't make it. It is so late at night, I...
C: I see. Have you got the address you are heading to?

P: Yes. Here it is. Shenlong Hotel.

C: Eh, Shenlong Hotel. It is a little far from here. Maybe you can take a DiDi, which is just like Uber in your country.

P: DiDi! Oh, yes. I have got the App in my phone. My friend has told me how to use it. Jesus! I forgot it. Thank you. It is so kind of you.

C: You are welcome! Have a nice stay here!

Activity 4: Please make up your own dialogue based on the following situation.

A woman passenger has just got out of a train. She takes a little baby and two big suitcases. A clerk is coming to offer help.

Conversation 3

Activity 1: Listen and answer.

1. What happened to the passenger?

2. Where did he buy the ticket?

Activity 2: Listen again and fill in the blanks.

1. Have you got the text message in your cell phone, _____?

2. Hmm, my device tells you did buy a ticket for _____, which arrived _____.

Activity 3: Work in pairs. Read the conversation at least twice, changing roles each time.

P: Excuse me, I can't find my ticket. I think I have lost it.

C: Have you got the text message in your cell phone, sent by 12306?

P: No. I bought it from the ticket office.

C: Then I need your ID Card.

P: OK. Here you are.

C: Hmm, my device tells you did buy a ticket for Train K118, which arrived 10 min ago.

P: Yes, that is it. Can I go out here now?

C: Sure. Take your ID Card back and have a nice day.

P: Thank you very much.

C: Not at all.

Activity 4:Please make up your own dialogue based on the fallowing situation.

A passenger is stopped by the clerk when he is trying to pass the exit.

What may be the problem? Think about it and make a dialogue with your partner.

 Words and Phrases ◀◀◀

be supposed to			应该
full fare			全票
original	[əˈrɪdʒənl]	adj.	原始的;最初的
balance	[ˈbæləns]	v.	使平衡;结算
Uber	[ˈjuːbə]	n.	优步(美国的一种打车App)
head to			去……地方
text message			短信
device	[dɪˈvaɪs]	n.	设备;装置
tell	[tel]	v.	显示;提示

 Section C:Passage Reading

Every exit is equipped with baffle gate. If your ticket is magnetic one, use the baffle gate, which will check your ticket automatically. Otherwise you should show your ticket to the staff member. If you want to transfer, please take the transfer access, which is also equipped with baffle gates. When getting off the train, you are required to exit immediately. Nobody is allowed to stay in the passageway.

 Words and Phrases ◀◀◀

baffle gate			闸机
magnetic	[mægˈnetɪk]	adj.	有磁性的
transfer access			换乘通道

 Exercises

Ⅰ. Terms translation

1. be equipped with
2. magnetic
3. baffle gate
4. transfer
5. staff member

II. Sentences translation

1. If your ticket is magnetic one, use the baffle gate, which will check your ticket automatically.

2. If you want to transfer, please take the transfer access, which is also equipped with baffle gates.

3. Nobody is allowed to stay in the passageway.

 Section D: Expanding View

Germany's ICE

In Germany, the high-speed train is called ICE, which is short for Inter-City Express. Currently there are 259 train sets in six different versions of the ICE vehicles in use, named ICE 1, ICE 2, ICE T, ICE 3 and ICE TD, ICE 4 (formerly named ICx). With the speed up to 300km/h, ICE is one of the fastest ways to travel between cities such as Berlin, Hamburg and Cologne. It connects all major cities in Germany, and also has international connections to Denmark, the Netherlands, Belgium, France, Switzerland and Austria.

Most ICE trains offer breakfast/lunch or dinner menus with many German specialties as well as snacks and a wide selection of beverages. In first class car, staff will serve food/drink to your seat. Folding bikes can be taken onboard. Non-folding bikes can be transported via the luggage courier service (this costs extra). Pets are permitted on ICE trains, but may be required to be kept in a traveling container or must wear a muzzle and a leash. Some ICE routes provide Wi-Fi.

Words and Phrases ◀◀◀

Inter-City Express			城际快车
trainset	[ˈtreinset]	n.	动车组
specialty	[ˈspeʃəltɪ]	n.	特产;招牌菜
beverage	[ˈbevərɪdʒ]	n.	饮料
reservation	[rezəˈveɪʃn]	n.	预订;保留
muzzle	[ˈmʌzl]	n.	口套
leash	[liːʃ]	n.	拴狗的绳子,皮带
version	[ˈvɜːʃn]	n.	版本

Section E: Self-evaluation

Ⅰ. Words and phrases translation

1. 售票厅
2. 行李认领
3. 地下停车场
4. 晚点
5. 全票
6. 补差价
7. 换票
8. 设备
9. 闸机
10. 转车

11. 工作人员

12. 换乘通道

13. 城际快车

14. 动车组

Ⅱ. Sentences translation

1. 这趟车两个小时前就该到了。

2. 把原始车票给售票人员，补完差价后就可以拿到新的车票。

3. 你可以打个滴滴过去，就像在你们国家乘坐优步车一样。

4. 你手机上有 12306 发送的购票信息吗？

5. 设备显示你的确购买了 K118 次列车的车票。

6. 每个出站口都设有自动闸机。

7. 下车后请立即出站。

8. 在一等座车厢，工作人员会将食物或饮料送到您的座位前。

9. 折叠自行车可以带上列车。

10. 一些 ICE 路线提供 Wi-Fi 服务。

Part I/Unit 7　Station Broadcasting

Unit 7

Station Broadcasting

Section A: Broadcasting

1. For faster service, use counters with a shorter queue. Passengers with Chinese second-generation ID Cards can purchase tickets at the ticket vending machines. Passengers from abroad, please present your passports and buy tickets from Ticket Counters.

2. Platform tickets are not available for CRH(China Railway High-speed) trains. For all other trains, a valid train ticket must be presented. Only one platform ticket is available per valid train ticket.

3. Your ticket is only valid for the designated train on your date of travel. You must rebook if you wish to change to an earlier or a later train. Only valid ticket holders may board the train.

4. Please present your ticket and matching ID Card. Boarding will be denied to passengers whose documents do not match. Thank you for your cooperation.

5. Dangerous items are strictly prohibited at stations or on trains.

6. Please check your train number and its boarding gate on the LED screen. And mind your belongings whilst waiting for the train.

7. Attention please! Train C2002 from Tianjin will arrive at Beijing South Station on Platform 2. Staffs in concerned area please get yourselves ready to receive the train.

8. Ladies and gentlemen, attention, please. The station announces the boarding of Train T153 for Shenyang. Passengers for this train please get your tickets ready and go to Boarding Gate 5. And please make sure nothing left behind in the waiting lounge. Thank you.

9. Use only one blue ticket at one time when using auto gates. Use auto gates if you have a blue magnetic ticket. Let station staff check your ticket if you have a red / pink non-magnetic one.

10. Dear passengers, train K389, from Chengdu to Fuzhou, will depart in 3min. For your safety, the ticket gate is closed now. If you missed it, please change your ticket at the ticket office. Thank you for your cooperation.

11. Attention, please! Train T75 to Lanzhou is leaving in no time. Please get on the train

immediately. If you have been on board, please make sure you are holding the right ticket. Platform ticket holders who have come to see people off are requested to get off the train right away and stay behind the white safety line on the platform. Thank you.

12. For your safety, please do not run on the platform. Thank you.

13. Please look after your children, and mind the gap between the train and the platform.

14. Please take care of seniors and children travelling with you.

15. For your safety, please wait behind the safety line.

 Words and Phrases

ticket vending machines			自动售票机
valid	[ˈvælɪd]	adj.	有效的;合法的
corresponding	[ˌkɒrəˈspɒndɪŋ]	adj.	相应的
boarding gates			检票口
prohibit	[prəˈhɪbɪt]	v.	禁止;阻止
CRH(China Railway High-speed)			中国高速铁路
concerned	[kənˈsɜːnd]	adj.	有关的;相关的
announce	[əˈnaʊns]	v.	播报;宣布
auto gates			自动检票机
depart	[dɪˈpɑːt]	v.	离开;出发
senior	[ˈsiːniə(r)]	n.	年长者

 Section B: Expanding View

Hyperloop is a new type of vehicle with the theoretical core of "vacuum steel pipe transportation". It has the characteristics of ultra-high speed, high safety, low energy consumption, low noise, and low pollution. Because of its capsule-shaped appearance, it is also called capsule high-speed rail.

The idea of "vacuum pipe transportation" was originally proposed by mechanical engineer Darryl Oster in the 1990s, and in 1997 he patented the technology. Elon Musk, CEO of Tesla, known as "tech madman", enriched the idea and proposed the new concept of "super high-speed railway", contributing more design details to this new type of transportation.

On May 12th, 2017, Hyperloop One first fully tested its super high-speed railway technology in a vacuum environment, using magnetic levitation technology to achieve a speed of 113km, and the test speed in July reached 310km.

On August 29th, 2017, China Aerospace Science & Industry Corp. announced in Wuhan had launched a research and development project for "a high-speed flight train" with a speed of 1000km/h. The super high-speed train with a maximum operating speed of 2000km and 4000km will be developed in the future.

In April 2018, Elon Musk announced that his "Super High Speed Railway Passenger Cabin" would be tested with a target speed of half the speed of sound and complete the brakes within 1.2km.

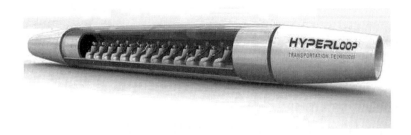

Words and Phrases

Hyperloop	[ˈhaɪpəluːp]	n.	超级高铁
theoretical	[θɪəˈretɪkl]	adj.	理论的
capsule	[ˈkæpsjuːl]	n.	胶囊；太空舱
vacuum	[ˈvækjʊəm]	n.	真空
patent	[ˈpænt]	n.	专利
		v.	取得……专利
magnetic levitation			磁悬浮
announce	[əˈnaʊns]	v.	宣布
brake	[breɪk]	n.	制动
		v.	制动

Section C: Self-evaluation

Ⅰ. Words and phrases translation

1. 二代身份证
2. 自动售票机
3. 动车组
4. 站台票
5. 危险物品
6. 屏幕
7. 接车
8. 候车室
9. 自动检票机

10. 检票口

11. 发车

12. 站台

13. 超级高铁

14. 真空

15. 磁悬浮

Ⅱ. Sentences translation

1. 持二代身份证的旅客,可以使用自动售票机购票。请外籍旅客持护照到售票厅的人工售票处购票。

2. 每张车票限售一张站台票。

3. 请您持车票和与票面信息相符的本人有效证件进站,乘车。

4. 候车时请注意保管好携带的行李、物品。

5. 请做好接车准备。

6. 请携带好您的行李物品,以免遗忘在候车室内。

7. 持蓝色车票旅客请使用自动检票机。

8. 来不及检票上车的旅客,请您到售票厅办理改签手续。

9. 注意站台与列车间的空隙。

10. 请在白色安全线以内排队等候,以免发生意外。

11. "超级高铁"是一种以"真空钢管运输"为理论核心的新型交通工具。

12. 中国航天科工公司在武汉宣布,已启动时速1000千米"高速飞行列车"的研发项目。

Part II

Train Service（列车服务）

铁路客运服务英语

Unit 8

Equipment Introduction

 Section A: Starting Out

Look at the following pictures and try to guess what they are.

```
second class seat        electric water-heater    driver's cabin
power socket             first class seat         business class seat
toilet                   luggage closet
```

1. _____

2. _____

3. _____

4. _____

Part II/Unit 8   Equipment Introduction

5. _____   6. _____

7. _____   8. _____

Section B: Listening and Speaking

SETTING: A PASSENGER IS ASKING FOR INFORMATION. (P = PASSENGER, C = CLERK)

Conversation 1

Activity 1: Listen and answer.
1. Where is the electric water-heater?
2. How to use the electric water-heater?

Activity 2: Listen again and fill in the blanks.
1. Just press the _____ and here comes _____.
2. There is something _____ temporarily.

Activity 3：Work in pairs. Read the conversation at least twice, changing roles each time.

P：Excuse me, where can I get hot water?

C：Electric water-heater is at the end of this carriage. Please follow me. Here it is.

P：How to use the electric water-heater?

C：Just press the red button and here comes the water. The water is hot, please be careful.

P：Thank you! Let me have a try. What's the matter with this heater? I can't get any water.

C：I am sorry. There is something wrong with it temporarily. Please fetch water from the next carriage.

P：Thank you. By the way, can I buy any tea on the train?

C：Yes. The train attendants will serve you with mobile vending carts.

P：That's great. Thank you.

C：You are welcome.

Activity 4：Please make up your own dialogue with the given information.

A passenger wants to get some hot water to drink, please help him.

Conversation 2

Activity 1：Listen and answer.

1. What kind of seat does the passenger like?

2. How can we make the seat more comfortable?

Activity 2：Listen again and fill in the blanks.

1. I've found you a seat _____ and it is _____ in that way.

2. The train can reach a top speed of _____. The window is made of _____, so you wouldn't feel dizzy.

Activity 3：Work in pairs. Read the conversation at least twice, changing roles each time.

P：Excuse me, could I have a window seat and face forward?

C：Sir, I've found you a seat by the window and it is No. 9 in that way.

P：Thank you so much, but how can I make the seat more comfortable?

C：That's easy. Please press the button on the armrest and against the seat at the same time.

Part II/Unit 8 Equipment Introduction

P: I did it, thank you. By the way, what's the highest speed of this train? It's running so fast.

C: The train can reach a top speed of 300km/h. The window is made of decelerating glass, so you wouldn't feel dizzy.

P: I see. Thank you very much.

C: My pleasure.

Activity 4: Please make up your own dialogue based on the following situation.

A passenger feels a little cold, and he is asking the crew for help.

Conversation 3

Activity 1: Listen and answer.

1. What did the passenger hang on the hook by the window?

2. Where can passenger put the large luggage in?

Activity 2: Listen again and fill in the blanks.

1. I'm afraid it's _____ to hang it on _____. Besides, the hook is for _____, and so on.

2. It might _____ from the _____ at any time.

Activity 3: Work in pairs. Read the conversation at least twice, changing roles each time.

C: Excuse me, whose handbag is this?

P: It's mine. What's the matter?

C: I'm afraid it's not safe to hang it on the hook by the window. Besides, the hook is for caps, coats, towels, and so on.

P: Thank you for your advice.

C: (To another passenger) Excuse me, sir. Whose suitcase is this?

P: It's mine. Do you want to open it for security check?

C: No, you misunderstood. It might fall down from the luggage rack at any time. It's dangerous. I suggest you take it down and put it in the luggage closet between two carriages.

P: Thank you very much. You are so considerate.

C: Don't mention it. Let me help you.

Activity 4:Please create your own dialogue with the following words and expressions.

Suppose you are the train attendant, a passenger wants to use the toilet. You may use the following words: be occupied, wait a moment, flush button, press, tap, induction.

Words and Phrases

electric water-heater			电热水炉
temporarily	[ˌtempəˈrerɪlɪ]	adv.	临时地
forward	[ˈfɔːwəd]	adv.	向前
decelerate	[ˌdiːˈseləreɪt]	v.	(使)减速
carriage	[ˈkærɪdʒ]	n.	客车厢
button	[ˈbʌtn]	n.	按钮
fetch	[fetʃ]	v.	取来
armrest	[ˈɑːmrest]	n.	扶手
considerate	[kənˈsɪdərət]	adj.	体贴的;考虑周到的
occupied	[ˈɒkjʊpaɪd]		已占用的;使用中的

Section C:Passage Reading

Why Smoking is Banned on Chinese Bullet Trains?

There are 4 main reasons for why smoking is banned on China high- speed trains:

1. Normally, the running speed of bullet trains is between 200km/h and 350km/h. The high running speed can bring extra difficulty to the fire rescue. Thus, when fires do happen, they are way more destructive than would otherwise be the case.

2. Currently, all types of high-speed trains are equipped with smoke detectors in the toilets. All the detectors are connected to the automatic shutdown system. So that once the smoke alarms are triggered, the system will carry out emergency braking to reduce the speed or to stop the train. This may cause late arrivals or even serious accidents.

3. To reduce the wind noise and air resistance, the carriages are fully closed. The good airtightness will make the smoke diffuse inside the carriages. This will not only make other passengers feel uncomfortable, but also will trigger the detector in the toilet.

4. High-speed trains are public transportations. Smoking on public transportations is not merely bad for your own health, but even worse to other passengers in the carriages.

In conclusion, smoking ban on high speed trains is for the safety and health of all the passengers.

Part II/Unit 8　Equipment Introduction

动车禁烟　安全你我他

Words and Phrases

rescue	[ˈreskjuː]	n.	救援
shutdown system			停车系统
resistance	[rɪˈzɪstəns]	n.	阻力
destructive	[dɪˈstrʌktɪv]	adj.	毁灭性的
trigger	[ˈtrɪɡə(r)]	v.	引发；触发
diffuse	[dɪˈfjuːs]	adj.	散开的

Exercises

I. Terms translation

1. fire rescue
2. public transportations
3. in conclusion
4. be banned
5. running speed
6. smoke detector

II. Sentence translation

1. The high running speed can bring extra difficulty to the fire rescue.
2. Currently, all types of high speed trains are equipped with smoke detectors in the toilets.
3. So that once the smoke alarms are triggered, the system will carry out emergency braking to reduce the speed or to stop the train.
4. To reduce the wind noise and air resistance, the carriages are fully closed.

Section D: Expanding View

Facilities on China High-Speed Trains

China high-speed train facilities include western-style toilets, luggage racks for regular suitcases and bags, luggage closets for large or heavy stuff, dining cars, and food trolley selling snacks. Being advanced, modern and clean, they ensure passengers a comfortable and pleasant China high-speed train ride.

Luggage Racks

Luggage racks are above the seats on both sides of a carriage. Only bags or suitcases of normal sizes can be put onto the racks; at the junctions of two carriages, there are luggage closets. The closets are usually over 1m high and is enough for a 30inch (76.2cm) suitcase. There are also rooms for 28inch (71.12cm) suitcases and other luggage at the back of the last row of seats in each carriage.

Dining Carriages

Food and drink are provided in the dining carriages. Only pre-packed meals are available, and these meals need to be heated in a microwave. The price goes from 15 yuan to 45 yuan. There are varieties of drinks for passengers to choose, including wine, beer, Coca-cola, juice, milk and coffee. The attendants will also push a trolley to sell packed food and snacks during a trip. Passengers in the business (sightseeing) class, super class and first-class carriages will be served with free meals and beverages.

Drinkable Hot Water

Each carriage has a water heater at the end. Free boiled water is available during the whole trip. The green indicator shows that the water is fully heated. Put your bottle under the tap and push the button, and you will get hot water. Disposable paper cups are available sometimes.

Wash Basins

The wash basins are either inside or outside of the toilets and some trains have warm water. Hand sanitizer and paper towels are provided.

Power Sockets

Long journey can often be boring and passengers like to take along laptops or mobile which depend on batteries. For your convenience, you will find that these batteries can be re-charged from sockets under the aisle-side seats in almost all carriages.

Internet

Free Wi-Fi is available on some trains. Therefore, as long as you have a smart phone or a laptop, you can surf the internet freely.

Entertainment

Each carriage has LCD TV (Liquid Crystal Display Television) sets playing movies or TV programs during a trip. The headset jacks and volume buttons are on the arm of each seat. Passengers can also listen to the radio when running in cities. Passengers in Business Class Seats also have their independent LCD TV screens, which are located in the left armrests of the seats.

Words and Phrases ◂◂◂

stuff	[stʌf]	n.	材料;原料
suitcase	[ˈsuːtkeɪs]	n.	手提箱
indicator	[ˈɪndɪkeɪtə(r)]	n.	指示器
sanitizer	[ˈsænɪtaɪzə]	n.	消毒剂
battery	[ˈbætrɪ]	n.	电池
junction	[ˈdʒʌŋkʃn]	n.	结合点
beverage	[beˈvərɪdʒ]	n.	饮料
disposable	[dɪˈspəʊzəbl]	adj.	一次性的
laptop	[ˈlæptɒp]	n.	便携式电脑
headset jacks			耳机塞孔

Section E: Self-evaluation

I. Words and phrases translation

1. 电热水炉
2. 按钮
3. 扶手
4. 减速

5. 救援

6. 停车系统

7. 阻力

8. 公共交通

9. 烟雾探测器

10. 材料

11. 手提箱

12. 饮料

13. 指示器

14. 一次性的

15. 耳机塞

16. 电池

17. 结合点

18. 消毒剂

Ⅱ. Sentences translation

1. 高铁列车是全车禁烟的。

2. 我来给你介绍一下车厢的设备设施吧？

3. 靠背可以调整得舒服些，按钮在这里。

4. 座椅网带内备有杂志、清洁袋、服务指南，请您自助使用。

5. 小桌板在侧扶手内，我来帮您打开。

6. 车厢两端为感应式端门，在您通过时会自动开启。

7. 空调设备没有问题，假如您觉得冷，我可以为您把温度调高点。

8. 每节车厢的连接处都设有紧急停车按钮，请您不要触碰，以免引发停车事故。

9. 乘客

10. 高速铁路

Unit 9

Welcoming Aboard

Section A: Starting Out

Look at the following signs of railway transportation and try to guess what they are.

CRH train	Crew room	Left luggage
Berth	First class seat	Aisle

1. _____

2. _____

3. _____

4. _____

5. _____   6. _____

Section B: Listening and Speaking

SETTING: IN THE CARRIAGE, A PASSENGER IS ASKING FOR INFORMATION. (*P* = *PASSENGER*, *C* = *CLERK*)

Conversation 1

Activity 1: Listen and answer.

1. Where are they?
2. Where is the correct carriage?

Activity 2: Listen again and fill in the blanks.

1. Would you please _____?
2. Please go along this way, referring _____.

Activity 3: Work in pairs. Read the conversation at least twice, changing roles each time.

C: Welcome to our train! Good morning, sir. Would you please show me your ticket?
P: Of course. Here you are.
C: Thank you for your cooperation. Sorry, this is Car No. 2. Your seat is in Car No. 4. Please go along this way, referring to the car number. You won't miss it.
P: I see. It's very kind of you. Thank you very much.
C: It's my pleasure.

Activity 4: Please make up your own dialogue with the given information.

A passenger gets on the wrong carriage, and he is asking how to get to the right carriage.

Conversation 2

Activity 1: Listen and answer.

1. What's the matter with the passenger?
2. How does the clerk help the passenger?

Activity 2: Listen again and fill in the blanks.

1. You are in Carriage 1, seat number _____.
2. That's very kind of you, but I think _____.

Activity 3: Work in pairs. Read the conversation at least twice, changing roles each time.

C: Welcome aboard!
P: Excuse me, where is my carriage?
C: Show me your ticket, please. You are in Carriage 1, seat number 2A, first class.
P: How can I get there?
C: Follow me, please. I'll show you your seat.
P: Thanks.
C: That's OK. Can I help you with your luggage?
P: That's very kind of you, but I think I can manage.
C: Here it is. But your luggage is too big. Could you please put it in the left luggage?
P: OK. Thank you.

Activity 4: Please make up your own dialogue with the given information.

A passenger gets on the train, but he can't find his seat. He is asking clerk for help.

Conversation 3

Activity 1: Listen and answer.

1. What's the matter with the passenger?
2. What should the passenger do if he wants to buy a berth ticket?

Activity 2: Listen again and fill in the blanks.

1. Could I buy _____ after I get on train?
2. Then you ask _____ for a berth ticket.

Activity 3: Work in pairs. Read the conversation at least twice, changing roles each time.

> C: Good afternoon, sir. Welcome aboard!
> P: Excuse me, how can I get to carriage No.9?
> C: Show me your ticket, please.
> P: Here you are.
> C: Your seat number is No.45 of Carriage 9. Please go ahead and pass the next carriage and your seat is in the middle of the carriage.
> P: Thanks. By the way, could I buy a berth ticket after I get on the train?
> C: Yes. If there is a vacant berth after the train leaves the station.
> P: What shall I do now?
> C: Well. First you board the train and get into Carriage No.10. Then you ask the conductor for a berth ticket.
> P: OK. Thank you.

Activity 4: Please make up your own dialogue with the given information.

A passenger gets on the train, but he can't find his seat. He is asking clerk for help in the carriage.

Words and Phrases ◂◂◂

crew room			乘务员室
aisle	[aɪl]	n.	过道;通道
cooperation	[kəʊˌɒpəˈreɪʃn]	n.	合作
vacant	[ˈveɪkənt]	adj.	空着的;未被占用的
refer	[rɪˈfɜː(r)]	v.	关于
first class seat			一等座
conductor	[kənˈdʌktə(r)]	n.	售票员
left luggage			行李寄存
berth ticket			卧铺票

 Section C: Passage Reading

China's high-speed trains to offer more smart services

The G7 Fuxing bullet train departed the Beijing South Railway Station in Beijing, capital of China, July 1st, 2018. China high-speed trains are expected to offer more smart services as the network continues to be upgraded with Internet technology.

A joint venture was officially launched on Thursday by China Railway Investment Co. Ltd., Zhejiang Geely Holding Group and Tencent to develop and operate an integrated platform that will provide Wi-Fi services to high-speed railway customers across China.

China Railway Gecent Technology Co. Ltd., with Geely and Tencent taking a combined 49% stake, will offer Wi-Fi connection, entertainment and leisure services, news and information, online catering and shopping, and other smart services.

"The integration of high-speed railway networks and the Internet can nurture a digital economy service platform and make trains part of cities' smart transport, tourism and retail," said Tencent board chairman and CEO Pony Ma.

China high-speed railways have attained a total of 25000km and are expected to reach 35000km by 2020, covering over 80% of cities with a population of more than 1 million.

 Words and Phrases ◂◂◂

bullet	[ˈbʊlɪt]	n.	子弹
upgrade	[ˌʌpˈgreɪd]	v.	升级
venture	[ˈventʃə(r)]	n.	企业；商业
launch	[lɔːntʃ]	v.	发动；开展
platform	[ˈplætfɔːm]	n.	平台；站台
leisure	[ˈleʒə(r)]	adj.	闲暇的
cater	[ˈkeɪtə(r)]	v.	提供饮食及服务
retail	[ˈriːteɪl]	n.	零售业
attain	[əˈteɪn]	v.	达到；得到
population	[ˌpɒpjuˈleɪʃn]	n.	人口

Exercises

I. Terms translation

1. bullet train
2. smart services
3. high-speed railway
4. a total of link with

II. Sentence translation

1. The G7 Fuxing bullet train departed the Beijing South Railway Station in Beijing, capital of China, July 1st, 2018.

2. China's high-speed trains are expected to offer more smart services as the network continues to be upgraded with Internet technology.

3. China's high-speed railways attained a total of 25000km and are expected to reach 35000km by 2020, covering over 80% of cities with a population of more than 1 million.

Section D: Expanding View

China Railway

China railway, especially its high-speed railway, is experiencing mushroom growth. Train has been one of the favorite means of transport for most Chinese people at present. Nearly 2.8 billion railway passenger trips were made throughout China in 2016, and the number has been growing at a rate of about 10% annually in recent years.

Generally speaking, China railway industry has gone through three stages of development. The first stage was from the late Qing period to 1948 where only a few railways were built and in use. It was regrettable that the introduction of railways to China was strongly rejected by the Qing government. At that time, the railway was considered as a scheme that would destroy the military defense, farmlands and Feng Shui of the Qing Empire. In 1876, the first railway in China, Wusong Railway, was put into operation without the permission of the Qing government. Since then, several railways were built in China, but most of them were constructed and controlled by Western powers.

The second stage was from 1949 to 2008, and large-scale construction was characteristic of this stage. Since the founding of the People's Republic of China, the country began to construct railways and develop railway industry in a planned way. In this period, a large number of old lines had been restored and improved, and lots of new lines had been built. Consequently, China's railroad network had been formed and expanded rapidly.

The third stage began in 2008, which marked the advent of the era of high-speed railway. High-speed lines were gradually replacing old busy ordinary-speed lines, greatly increasing transport capacity and making train travel much easier than before. In 2017, Fuxing trains started to run between Beijing and Shanghai at a speed of 350km/h, which made them the world's fastest commercial high-speed trains.

 Words and Phrases ◂◂◂

mushroom	[ˈmʌʃrʊm]	adj.	如蘑菇般迅速发展
passenger	[ˈpæsɪndʒə(r)]	n.	乘客
reject	[rɪˈdʒekt]	v.	拒绝
scheme	[skiːm]	n.	计划；诡计
military	[ˈmɪlətri]	adj.	军事的
defense	[dɪˈfens]	v.	防御
large-scale	[lɑːdʒ skeɪl]	adj.	大规模的
railway network			铁路网
characteristic	[ˌkærəktəˈrɪstɪk]	n.	特征；特色
restore	[rɪˈstɔː(r)]	v.	恢复
advent	[ˈædvent]	n.	出现；到来
replace	[rɪˈpleɪs]	v.	替换
capacity	[kəˈpæsəti]	n.	能力
commercial	[kəˈmɜːʃl]	adj.	商业的
high-speed railway			高速铁路
transport capacity			运输能力

Section E: Self-evaluation

I. Words and phrases translation

1. 一等座
2. 售票员
3. 大件行李
4. 卧铺票
5. 中国高铁
6. 升级
7. 子弹头列车
8. 智能服务
9. 拒绝
10. 计划
11. 军事的
12. 防御
13. 大规模的
14. 典型的
15. 恢复
16. 铁路网
17. 运输能力

II. Sentences translation

1. 欢迎您乘坐本次列车！
2. 请把您的车票给我看一下。
3. 谢谢您的配合。
4. 请您顺着车厢号走，一定能找到。
5. 您是在1号车厢，一等座2A号。
6. 请跟我来。我领您到座位上去。
7. 请您将行李放在大件行李存放处，好吗？
8. 请问9号车厢怎么走？
9. 请问上车后可以购买卧铺票吗？
10. 您可以先上车，去10号车厢，然后向列车长请求买一张卧铺票。
11. 这列车是CRH 3型列车，引进德国西门子技术。
12. CRH 3型列车设有1辆一等车，7辆二等车(含1辆餐车)，全列车定员557人。

Part II/Unit 10 Service in the Carriage

Unit 10

Service in the Carriage

Section A: Starting Out

Look at the following signs of railway transportation and try to guess what they are.

```
train counter              dinning car
seat pocket                train cab
```

1. _____

2. _____

3. _____

4. _____

 Section B:Listening and Speaking

SETTING:IN THE CARRIAGE, A PASSENGER IS ASKING FOR INFORMATION. (P = PASSENGER,C = CLERK)

Conversation 1

Activity 1:Listen and answer.

1. What's the next station?

2. How long will the train stay there?

Activity 2:Listen again and fill in the blanks.

1. _____. What's the next _____?

2. Be sure to get on the train as soon as _____.

Activity 3:Work in pairs. Read the conversation at least twice, changing roles each time.

P:Excuse me. What's the next station?
C:It's Shanghai.
P:How long will the train stay there?
C:8 minutes.
P:Can I have a walk on the platform?
C:Of course, but please do not go too far. Be sure to get on the train as soon as the bell rings.
P:All right. Thank you.
C:You are welcome.

Activity 4:Please make up your own dialogue with the given information.

A passenger will go to Guangzhou, but he doesn't know how long the train will stay at the platform. He is asking something about it in the carriage.

Conversation 2

Activity 1:Listen and answer.

1. Does the train have Internet access?

Part II/Unit 10 Service in the Carriage

2. Where could the passenger charge his cell phone in the carriage?

Activity 2: Listen again and fill in the blanks.

1. We do not provide _____ on the train.

2. There is a _____ under the _____.

Activity 3: Work in pairs. Read the conversation at least twice, changing roles each time.

P: Excuse me, sir. Dose the train have Internet access?

C: Oh, sorry. We do not provide the Internet service on the train.

P: As far as I know, many Inter-City and direct express trains have already providing Wi-Fi service since 2015.

C: You are right. Only Beijing Railway Bureau have installed free Wi-Fi on over 100 trains, but the bullet trains are not included.

P: What a pity! Hope to use it on the high-speed trains as soon as possible.

C: Wi-Fi service is expected to be offered on China's high-speed trains in three to five years.

P: That's great. By the way, where could I charge my cell phone in the carriage?

C: There is a socket under each aisle seat.

P: Thank you.

C: You are welcome.

Activity 4: Please make up your own dialogue with the given information.

A passenger gets on the train, but he can't find his seat. He is asking something about it in the carriage.

Conversation 3

Activity 1: Listen and answer.

1. Where is the toilet on the train?

2. Is it allowed to smoke on the CRH Train? Why?

Activity 2: Listen again and fill in the blanks.

1. It seems that it is occupied for quite _____.

2. _____ the alarm goes off, the train will stop _____.

Activity 3:Work in pairs. Read the conversation at least twice, changing roles each time.

P:Excuse me. Is there any toilet in this carriage?

C:Yes, there is a toilet at the end of the carriage.

P:Why is it locked now? It seems that it is occupied for quite a while.

C:I am afraid all the toilets are locked now.

P:Why?

C:Because the train is approaching a station. Toilets on the train are not supposed to be used when it stops at a station.

P:Oh, I see. How long will the train stay at the station?

C:10minutes. I'm afraid you have to wait a moment. The toilet will be available when the train departs.

P:OK. Thanks. By the way, is there a smoking compartment? Where can I smoke?

C:Sorry, smoking is not allowed on CRH train.

P:But I can smoke in a restricted area between two cars on an ordinary train.

C:Yes. But smoking onboard CRH train is dangerous, and it may set off a fire. Smoke alarms are installed throughout the entire train, and they are sensitive enough to detect any tiny amount of smoke. Once the alarm goes off, the train will stop automatically. In that case, it will delay the arrival time.

P:I see. Thank you for your explanation.

C:It is my pleasure.

Activity 4:Please make up your own dialogue with the given information.

A passenger gets on the train, and he wanders where the toilet is. He is asking something about it in the carriage.

 Words and Phrases ◂◂◂

platform	[ˈplætfɔːm]	n.	平台;站台
seat number			座位号
approach	[əˈprəʊtʃ]	v.	接近
occupy	[ˈɒkjʊpaɪ]	v.	占领;使用
depart	[dɪˈpɑːt]	v.	离开
set off			引起
go off			突然大作
install	[ɪnˈstɔːl]	v.	安装
automatically	[ˌɔːtəˈmætɪklɪ]	adv.	自动地

lock	[lɒk]	v.	锁
suppose	[sə'pəʊz]	v.	假定
available	[ə'veɪləbl]	adj.	可获得的
compartment	[kəm'pɑːtmənt]	n.	隔间
alarm	[ə'lɑːm]	n.	警报
sensitive	['sensətɪv]	adj.	灵敏的
delay	[dɪ'leɪ]	v.	延迟

Section C: Passage Reading

Smoking Violators to Get 180-day Train Travel Ban

Starting in May, 2018, passengers who smoke on high-speed trains or in smoke-free zones of other trains will be prevented from train travel for 180 days, according to a released document. The document was jointly issued by the National Development and Reform Commission, the Supreme People's Court and other government departments.

If passengers steal a ride, buy tickets with fake ID Cards, or board trains with invalid tickets, they will not be allowed to buy tickets again unless they pay a fee equal to the ticket costs.

If the same situation happens three times within the year after a previous fee payment, they have to wait 90 days before buying tickets again, and only after paying all outstanding fees.

A roster of those banned from taking trains will be publicized on 12306.cn, a ticket booking website, and credit china.gov.cn, a credit check website, for 7 consecutive days from the first day of each month. Those listed can appeal during that period.

 Words and Phrases ◀◀◀

violator	[ˈvaɪəleɪtə(r)]	n.	违反者
ban	[bæn]	n.	禁令
		v.	禁止
release	[rɪˈliːs]	v.	发布
document	[ˈdɒkjumənt]	n.	公文；文档
fake	[feɪk]	adj.	伪造的
invalid	[ɪnˈvælɪd]	adj.	无效的
equal	[ˈiːkwəl]	adj.	相等的；平等的
previous	[ˈpriːviəs]	adj.	之前的
outstanding	[aʊtˈstændɪŋ]	adj.	未完成的
roster	[ˈrɒstə(r)]	n.	花名册

 Exercises

Ⅰ. Terms translation

1. smoke-free zones
2. prevent from
3. according to
4. steal a ride
5. invalid tickets

Ⅱ. Sentence translation

1. Starting in May, 2018, passengers who smoke on high-speed trains or in smoke-free zones of other trains will be prevented from train travel for 180 days, according to a released document.

2. If passengers steal a ride, buy tickets with fake ID Cards, or board trains with invalid tickets, they will not be allowed to buy tickets again unless they pay a fee equal to the ticket costs.

 Section D: Passage Reading

Seat Classes on Trains

Besides travelling by air, travelling by train is also a popular choice for people who need to take trips in China. There are 8 kinds of classes available on trains in China.

No.1 First-class Seat

First-class seat is equipped on the bullet train only. The facilities are designed according to the first-class seat on European high-speed trains and business-class seat on flight, so it got the name.

The price of first-class seat is the most expensive one among the common used scheduled trains. While if you are looking for a deluxe comfortable experience, this type of seat is a great choice for you.

No. 2　Second-class Seat

Second-class seat is equipped on the bullet train only. The facilities are designed according to the second-class seat on European high-speed trains and economy-class seat on flight, so it got the name. For people who choose high-speed train in China, second-class seat can take into consideration because of the great comfortable feeling and less cost than the first-class seat.

No. 3　Soft Sleeper

Four berths in a compartment, two uppers and two lowers. The soft sleeper can be a good choice if you take an overnight train or a long-distance train. The soft berth ensures a good sleeping quality than any other type. And each compartment has a secure door that locks and small space for baggage. One thing that we should pay attention to is that toilets and a common washroom are located at both ends of the sleeping car and Western-style and pit toilets are typically include.

No. 4 Hard Sleeper

Six couchettes in each compartment, two uppers, two middles and two lowers. No secured door for each compartment, so it may be noisy and no private room for you to have a sleep. Many people would like to choose this type for long-distance travel because it is cheaper than the soft sleeper. Another thing we should let you know is that pit toilets and a common washroom are located at the end of the sleeping car. Better to avoid buying Hard Sleeper ticket because of the dirty toilets and noisy carriages.

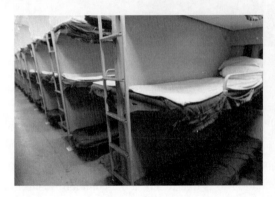

Part II/Unit 10 Service in the Carriage

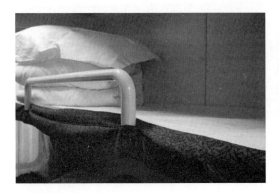 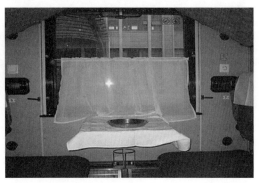

No. 5 Soft Seat

Carriages of soft seat are equipped with cushioned-seats and wider room on the carriages. They are cleaner and less crowded than the hard seat carriages with a slightly more expensive price than the hard one. Less people will choose this type so it ensures the comparative quietness in the carriages.

No. 6 Hard Seat

Carriages of hard seat may be the least comfortable one. Hard seat on some short-distance trains will be better than the long-distance ones. Because it is the cheapest one, so more people would like to choose this type. But hard seat carriages will be noisier, more crowded and dirtier than other level carriages.

No. 7 Business-class Seat

This type may only be found in some G-and D-trains only. 24 red seats with 180° turning and bed-transforming functions are equipped in. 3 seats in a row divided into single seat and twin seat two kinds. A screen to prevent passenger disturbing from others ensures a private room for each other.

No. 8 Deluxe soft sleeper

The deluxe soft sleeper is totally deluxe with the extremely special equipment. These sleeping cars have just two berths per compartment—one upper and one lower—also boast a private Western-style toilet and separate sitting area. Each compartment has a secure door that locks and small space for luggage.

Words and Phrases

first-class seat	一等座
second-class seat	二等座
soft sleeper	软卧

hard sleeper			硬卧
equip	[ɪˈkwɪp]	v.	装备
berth	[bɜːθ]	n.	卧铺
soft seat			软座
hard seat			硬座
business-class seat			商务座
deluxe soft sleeper			豪华软卧
deluxe	[dəˈlʌks]	adj.	高级的;豪华的
cushion	[ˈkʊʃn]	v.	(用垫子)使柔和

Section E: Self-evaluation

Ⅰ. Words and phrases translation

1. 站台
2. 动车
3. 座位号
4. 接近
5. 离开
6. 隔间
7. 违反者
8. 发布
9. 公文
10. 伪造的
11. 平等的
12. 之前的
13. 吸烟区
14. 逃票
15. 无效票
16. 硬卧
17. 软座
18. 商务座

Ⅱ. Sentences translation

1. 打扰一下,请问下一站是哪里?
2. 列车会停靠多长时间?
3. 请问火车上能上网吗?
4. 据我所知,自 2015 年,许多城际和直达特快列车已经开始提供 Wi-Fi 服务。
5. Wi-Fi 服务将会在未来的三到五年应用在中国高铁上。

6. 请问在哪里可以给手机充电?
7. 每个外侧座位下都设有电源插座。
8. 请问有吸烟室吗?
9. 很抱歉,高铁列车上禁止吸烟。
10. 全车安装了烟雾探测器,一旦警报器响了,列车将会自动停车,这将耽误我们准时到达。

Part II/Unit 11 Dining Car Service

Unit 11

Dining Car Service

 Section A: Starting Out

Look at the following pictures and find out the right words for them.

box meal	food trolley	chips	biscuits
pistachio	beverage	popcorn	sunflower seeds
raisins	beef jerky		

1. _____

2. _____

3. _____

4. _____

5. _____

6. _____

7. _____

8. _____

9. _____

10. _____

Section B: Listening and Speaking

SETTING: IN THE DINING CAR, A PASSENGER IS ASKING FOR INFORMATION.
(P = PASSENGER, C = CLERK, D = DINING CAR CHIEF)

Part II/Unit 11 Dining Car Service

Conversation 1

Activity 1: Listen and answer.
1. Does the train have a dining car?
2. What kind of food will the passenger eat?

Activity 2: Listen again and fill in the blanks.
1. If you like _____, we have _____.
2. If you like _____, we have _____.

Activity 3: Work in pairs. Read the conversation at least twice, changing roles each time.

P: Excuse me. Do you offer meal on the train?

C: Yes, we do. After the train sets off, our attendants will serve you with mobile vending carts. You can also go to the dining car. Snacks, soft drinks, beers and box meals are sold in the dining car.

P: Thank you. By the way, can you tell me where the dining car is?

C: It's in carriage 8.

P: Thank you.

C: You are welcome. (In the dining car.)

P: Excuse me, what do you offer today?

D: Please take a look. If you like Chinese food, we have set meals and soups. If you like Western food, we have bread and milk. Which do you prefer?

P: A set meal and soup, please.

D: OK, a set meal and soup. Is there anything else you want to have?

P: No, thanks.

D: My pleasure. Please wait a second.

Activity 4: Please make up your own dialogue with the given information.

A passenger wants to buy something to drink, so he talks with the Dining Car Chief. You may use the following words: coffee, hot water, black tea, coke, orange juice, green tea.

Conversation 2

Activity 1: Listen and answer.
1. Which flavor do the passengers prefer?

2. What will they drink?

Activity 2: Listen again and fill in the blanks.

1. We serve almost _____. Here is the _____. Which one _____?

2. We heard that Sichuan cuisine is very famous, so _____.

Activity 3: Work in pairs. Read the conversation at least twice, changing roles each time.

> D: Good morning, sir. What can I do for you?
>
> P: I'd like to have lunch here.
>
> D: How many people, please?
>
> P: Four.
>
> D: Take a seat, please.
>
> P: What do you serve for lunch?
>
> D: We serve almost 10 kinds of meals. Here is the menu. Which one do you prefer?
>
> P: We heard that Sichuan cuisine is very famous, so we'd like to try some Sichuan foods. Hot foods are agreeable.
>
> D: OK. Kung Pao Chicken is a famous Sichuan dish in China with chicken and hot pepper as the ingredients.
>
> P: Great! We will try it. Four meals, please.
>
> D: OK. Would you like something to drink?
>
> P: Orange juice. Thank you.
>
> D: You are welcome. Please wait for a moment, you will be served soon.

Activity 4: Please create your own dialogue with the following words and expressions.

Two passengers want to have lunch in the dining car. The attendant in the dining car offer help to them by offering seats, recommending the menu such as western food, Chinese food, Sweet and Sour Fish, Scrambled Eggs, Tomato and Egg Soup.

Conversation 3

Activity 1: Listen and answer.

1. How much should the passenger pay for the breakfast?

2. What will the passengers eat?

Activity 2: Listen again and fill in the blanks.

1. I'm afraid _____.

2. We only accept _____. You can also pay with _____.

Activity 3: Work in pairs. Read the conversation at least twice, changing roles each time.

D: Good morning, can I help you?
P: Can we have breakfast now?
D: Yes, of course. Here is the menu.
P: Thank you. We will have 4 little buns, 2 bowls of dumplings and 2 bowls of beef with rice noodles.
D: 98 yuan.
P: I'm afraid there is a mistake here.
D: Let me check. (A few minutes later.) Sorry, it should be 88 yuan.
P: Do you accept checks?
D: Sorry, we don't. We only accept cash. You can also pay with Alipay or WeChat.
P: OK. Here is a 100-yuan bill.
D: Here is your change.
C: Thank you.

Activity 4: Please make up your own dialogue based on the following situation.

A passenger wants to have lunch in the dining car, so he asks you some information about the foods and prices.

 Words and Phrases ◀◀◀

offer	[ˈɒfə(r)]	v.	提供
vending	[ˈvendɪŋ]	v.	出售
snack	[snæk]	n.	快餐;点心
cuisine	[kwɪˈziːn]	n.	菜肴
bill	[bɪl]	n.	账单;钞票
mobile	[ˈməʊbaɪl]	adj.	可移动的
cart	[kɑːt]	n.	手推车
menu	[ˈmenjuː]	n.	菜单
bun	[bʌn]	n.	圆形小面包
cheque	[tʃek]	n.	支票

Section C: Passage Reading

Food Delivery Service on High-Speed Trains

Food delivery service is provided on high-speed trains passing by many cities including Shanghai, Tianjin, Nanjing, Guangzhou, Xi'an, Hangzhou, Shenyang, Wuhan, Changsha and Chengdu. However, the service is currently only available through the cell phone App of China Railway Corporation, which only has a Chinese version. If you have a Chinese friend, you can ask him or her to make a reservation for you, which should be made one hour prior to departure. You need to pay extra 8 yuan for delivery. Hopefully, the service will soon be available in English, too, so overseas passengers can have chances to taste the distinctive local foods of the cities along the way.

Words and Phrases

delivery	[dɪˈlɪvərɪ]	n.	递送；传送
currently	[ˈkʌrəntlɪ]	adv.	当前；目前
available	[əˈveɪləbl]	adj.	可获得的
make a reservation			订餐
prior to			在……之前
departure	[dɪˈpɑːtʃə]	n.	启程；离开

 **Exercises**

I. Terms translation

1. delivery service
2. pass by
3. make a reservation
4. prior to
5. be available
6. have a chance

II. Sentence translation

1. However, the service is currently only available through the cell phone App of China Railway Corporation, which only has a Chinese version.

2. Hopefully, the service will soon be available in English, too, so overseas passengers can have chances to taste the distinctive local foods of the cities along the way.

 Section D: Expanding View

Food on China train

When traveling on a China train, the food can be bought from the dining car, the food trolleys, and the platform vendors. The fare of the food is not included in the train ticket and only Chinese Yuan is accepted for payment. Food delivery service is also available on some high-speed trains.

Dining Car

A dining car (American English) or a restaurant car (British English), also a diner, is a railway passenger car that serves meals in the manner of a full-service, sit-down restaurant.

Most Chinese trains have a dining car (except some short-distance ones), which provides meals, drinks and snacks during a trip. A dining car is often at the carriage No. 9 on a normal train and carriage No. 4 or No. 5 on a high-speed one. Dining fare is not included in the ticket, so you need to pay for the food.

Food on board is usually Chinese style, and western food is usually not available. Breakfast usually includes porridge, pickles, boiled eggs, Chinese breads and steamed stuffed buns; sometimes, breads, teas and coffees are also available. For lunch and dinner, you can find rice with fried vegetables, soups and noodles. Available food on high-speed trains also include prepared and heated packed meals, and the prices range from 15 yuan to 45 yuan. In the dining car of non-high-speed trains, there is a kitchen and the chefs make dishes during the trip; passengers can order the dishes on the menu. As for drinks, beers, non-alcoholic beverages and bottled water are usually available. Popular snacks may also be purchased and include items such as sunflower seeds, peanuts, crackers, potato chips and vacuum packed braised food.

Trolleys

The seats in a dining car are limited 30 to 40, so there are railway attendants bringing trolleys through the carriages selling packed meals at meal times, which are the same rice, vegetables and noodles as those in the dining car. At other times, they also sell drinks, snacks, magazines and packed fruits.

Platform

Apart from the food on board, passengers can also buy food from the vendors at platform when the train stops at a station. Most food is simple, but sometimes you can get some really good local snacks better than the choice on board. These can be dishes such as braised duck necks, boiled corn cobs, tea flavored boiled eggs and rice noodles.

Words and Phrases

payment	[ˈpeɪmənt]	n.	付款
style	[staɪl]	n.	风格
porridge	[ˈpɔrɪdʒ]	n.	粥
pickle	[ˈpɪkəl]	n.	泡菜
range from			从……变化到
cracker	[ˈkrækə(r)]	n.	薄脆饼干

Section E: Self-evaluation

Ⅰ. Words and phrases translation

1. 餐车
2. 提供
3. 手推车
4. 快餐
5. 菜肴
6. 账单
7. 支票
8. 订餐
9. 可获得的
10. 启程
11. 站台
12. 售卖者
13. 付款
14. 粥
15. 车厢
16. 从……变化到
17. 服务员
18. 在……之前

Ⅱ. Sentences translation

1. 欢迎您到餐车用餐。
2. 能告诉我餐车在哪吗?
3. 对不起,我们不收外币。
4. 早上好!我帮您把小桌板打开,这是列车为您准备的茶水和咖啡,请慢用。
5. 如果您要用餐,我会及时通知餐车人员为您点餐并送餐。
6. 我们有可乐、橙汁、绿茶和咖啡。您需要哪一种?
7. 抱歉!因为运行时间比较短,车上没有配餐。餐车有休闲食品和饮料,希望合您口味。
8. 请问您是去餐车吗?
9. 餐车在 5 号车厢请您往前走。
10. 您需要哪一种茶?

铁路客运服务英语

Unit 12

Train Broadcasting

 Section A: Starting Out

Look at the following signs of railway transportation and try to guess what are they.

```
train broadcasting    folding table    train policeman    sanitary bag
```

1. _____

2. _____

3. _____

4. _____

Section B: Listening and Speaking

Pre-departure Announcement

1. Announcement for welcoming passengers.

All train crew members, attention, please. Passengers' tickets have been checked at the station. Please open the car doors to welcome passengers aboard.

2. Announcement that is broadcasted 5min before train's departure.

Dear passengers, this train K158 departs from Changchun. The departure time is 13:32. There is still 5 minutes for the train to leave. Those who get on a wrong train or come to see friends off, please get off the train in order to avoid any accident. Please don't shake hands with those on the platform when the train begins to move.

Post-departure Announcement

1. Departure Announcement.

Dear passengers! Accompanied by sound and happy music, Train Z62 departs from Changchun. Your journey and our train service work begin at the same time. Here, on behalf of all the crew, I would like to greet to you and hope you have a pleasant and safe journey.

2. Welcoming speech.

Good evening, ladies and gentlemen, welcome aboard! This is Train G48 from Harbin West Railway Station to Dalian North Railway station. My name is Liu Yang, head of the crew. On behalf of the crew, I wish you a pleasant trip.

The train is pulling of Harbin West Railway Station. It will arrive at Dalian North Railway station at 12:03, covering a distance of 921km. The trip will take 3 hours and 35 minutes with 2 stops before the terminal. We are from Harbin Railway Bureau. We are committed to creating an efficient and friendly environment. We offer you round-the-clock service.

3. Announcement for tidying carriages.

Dear passengers! In order to have a fine and tidy environment, please put your belongings on the luggage rack orderly and steadily. For those heavier or fragile luggage, please put them under your seat/berth. So that the carriage can be kept beautiful and tidy and also the safety of the articles can be ensured.

4. Announcement for ticket checking.

Dear passengers, if you haven't bought the tickets in time, please go to the chief conductor's desk to buy your tickets. It is in Car No. 10. Our working staff will go to each carriage to check your tickets. After you listen to the broadcasting, please return to your seats or berths to wait for the personnel's coming. Thanks for your cooperation.

5. Announcement for using berths.

Dear passengers, those who have berth tickets, please take a rest in your sleepers. Your tickets should be handed to the conductor to be kept together. Before you get off the train, please change berth tags for tickets. According to relevant railway regulations, sleeper ticket holders still haven't changed tickets for berth tags one hour after train's departure, your berths will be resold as vacant ones. So please handle it as soon as possible not to influence your rest.

Announcement on the Way

1. Station name prediction.

Dear passengers, attention, please. The next station is Changchun West Station. It is scheduled to arrive at 09:22. (But I'm sorry to inform you that the train is delayed about 4 minutes because the railway is being repaired. So the train will arrive at Changchun West Station at 09:26). This section covers 298km and will cost 54 minutes.

2. Announcement before arriving at station.

Dear passengers, the next station is Changchun West Station. If this is your station, please take your luggage and wait at both ends of the carriage. The train is about to arrive at Changchun West Station.

3. Announcement when arriving at station.

Dear passengers, the train is now stopping at Changchun West Station for 2 minutes. The platform is on the left side of the train's running direction. Please get off the train orderly and do not push.

4. Announcement for meal service.

Dear passengers, it is time for lunch. Now the dinning car begins to serve you. Those who want to have meals, please go to Car No. 9. Dining car attendants will serve you there.

5. Announcement for lost and found.

Attention, please, one passenger of this train lost his mobile phone accidentally. If someone finds it, please contact the announcement room. The announcement room is in Car No. 12. Thank you.

6. Emergency announcement.

Dear passengers, may I have your attention, please? Is there a doctor on the train? A passenger is suffering a heart attack, this is an emergency, and we need your help. please be quick and come to the sixth carriage. Thank you.

7. Announcement for looking for somebody.

Ladies and gentlemen, may I have your attention, please? A little boy named Peter from America, please go to the dining car. Your father is expecting you there. Thank you.

Arrival Announcement

1. Announcement before arriving at the terminal station.

Dear passengers, the terminal Beijing Station is arriving soon. Before the train's arrival, please cooperate with us again to keep the carriages clean. In order to make the train clean when arriving at the terminal, we'll make a clean sweep. When conductors do some cleaning beside you, please move your articles that are under your seat. After the carriages have been swept, please help us to keep them clean. Please forgive us for bringing you so much trouble when cleaning. In order to keep the terminal station clean, the toilets on the train will be locked in advance, so please use them ahead of time. Thank you for your cooperation.

2. Arrival announcement.

Dear passengers, with songs and laughter, our journey life is near the end. This Train Z64 departs from Changchun Station, travels around 9 hours and 17 minutes and will arrive at the terminal Beijing Station. On behalf of our train personnel, I shall express our thankfulness for your support to our work. And I hope that you can take our train next time. Hope we can meet again.

 Words and Phrases

sanitary	[ˈsænətrɪ]	adj.	卫生的;清洁的
announcement	[əˈnaʊnsmənt]	n.	宣告;通告
crew	[kruː]	n.	全体乘务员
departure	[dɪˈpɑːtʃə(r)]	n.	离开
accompany	[əˈkʌmpənɪ]	v.	陪伴;陪同
on behalf of			代表
terminal	[ˈtɜːmɪnl]	n.	终点站
efficient	[ɪˈfɪʃnt]	adj.	高效的
Harbin Railway Bureau			哈尔滨铁路局
round-the-clock			全天候的
fragile	[ˈfrædʒaɪl]	adj.	易碎的
schedule	[ˈʃedjuːl]	v.	安排
belonging	[bɪˈlɒŋɪŋ]	n.	附属品
accidentally	[ˌæksɪˈdentəlɪ]	adv.	偶然地;意外地
suffer	[ˈsʌfə(r)]	v.	遭受
emergency	[ɪˈmɜːdʒənsɪ]	n.	紧急情况
sweep	[swiːp]	n.	打扫
in advance			提前
thankfulness	[ˈθæŋkfʊlnəs]	n.	谢意

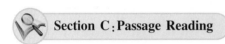

Section C: Passage Reading

Railway Passenger Transport Business—
from *Railway Law of the People's Republic of China*

All railway transport enterprises shall guarantee safe transports of passengers and goods and punctual train arrivals.

A railway transport contract shall be an agreement in which the mutual rights and obligations between the railway transport enterprise and the passenger (s) or shipper (s) are defined. A passenger ticket, a luggage, parcel or goods consignment note, shall represent a contract or a constituent part of a contract.

A railway transport enterprise shall ensure the information on the passengers' tickets, such as the arrival dates and the destinations. If the passengers can not get on the train on time due to the problems of railway transport enterprise, the enterprise will refund the total sum of the fare to passengers as the passengers' requirements, or make arrangements for the passengers to take another train to the same destination. A railway transport enterprise shall take effective measures to serve the passengers well in a courteous, warm and cultured manner, keep the station premises and passenger cars clean and sanitary, provide boiled drinking water and good catering services on the train. A railway transport enterprise shall take measures to protect the environment along railway lines from pollution.

Any passenger boarding a train shall hold a valid passenger ticket. Any passenger who get on a train without a ticket or with an invalid ticket shall pay the fare on the train plus additional charge as specified in relevant railway regulations; the railway transport enterprise may order any passenger who refuses to do so to leave the train.

 Words and Phrases ◂◂◂

punctual	[ˈpʌŋktʃʊəl]	adj.	准时的
mutual	[ˈmjuːtʃʊəl]	adj.	共同的;相互的
obligation	[ˌɒblɪˈɡeɪʃn]	n.	义务;责任
represent	[ˌreprɪˈzent]	v.	代表
constituent	[kənˈstɪtjʊənt]	adj.	组成的
courteous	[ˈkɜːtɪəs]	adj.	有礼貌的
cultured	[ˈkʌltʃəd]	adj.	文雅的
premises	[ˈpremɪsɪz]	n.	办公场所
catering	[ˈkeɪtərɪŋ]	n.	餐饮供应

Exercises

I. Terms translation

1. Railway transport enterprise
2. consignment note
3. due to

II. Sentences translation

1. All railway transport enterprises shall guarantee safe transports of passengers and goods and punctual train arrivals.

2. A railway transport enterprise shall ensure the passengers of riding on a train of the numbers and on the dates stated on the passengers' tickets, and of arriving at the destinations stated on the same tickets.

3. Any passenger boarding a train shall hold a valid passenger ticket.

4. The railway transport enterprise may order any passenger who refuses to do so to leave the train.

Section D: Expanding View

Luggage & Parcel Transportation

Checked luggage refers to clothing, books and other items for personal use, wheelchairs for the disabled are also included. Currency, securities, cultural relics, jewelry, important documents and other valuables are not allowed in checked luggage. The weight limit for each piece is 50kg. The outside size of your luggage is no more than 160cm, which is the sum of the length, width and height. Passengers can choose to transport checked luggage on the same train they are traveling on or it may be transported in advance. If it is transported on same train, it can be claimed as soon as you reach your destination. If it is checked in advance, it may arrive on a later train. Staff will notify you to come and pick it up after it has arrived. Remember to claim it as soon as possible after being informed, as the station will only keep it for free for 3 days, storage fee will be charged after that time.

Parcel refers to small loads which are suitable to transport in a luggage car. When you want to transport items which are restricted to transport by People's Republic of China, and items requiring inspection according to the government regulations, certain certificates should be presented.

Special note: explosive, dangerous items, compressed gases, flammable liquids, flammable solids and poisons are not allowed to bring into a train station or transport by train.

Words and Phrases

parcel	[ˈpɑːsl]	n.	包裹
personal	[ˈpɜːsənl]	adj.	个人的
currency	[ˈkʌrənsɪ]	n.	货币
security	[sɪˈkjʊərətɪ]	n.	安全
jewelry	[ˈdʒuːəlrɪ]	n.	珠宝
explosive	[ɪkˈspləʊsɪv]		易爆的
transport	[ˈtrænspɔːt]	n.	运输
destination	[ˌdestɪˈneɪʃn]	n.	目的地
notify	[ˈnəʊtɪfaɪ]	v.	通知
fee	[fiː]	n.	费用
load	[ləʊd]	n.	负载
suitable	[ˈsuːtəbl]	adj.	合适的
restrict	[rɪˈstrɪkt]	v.	限制
poison	[ˈpɔɪzn]	n.	毒药

Section E: Self-evaluation

Ⅰ. Words and phrases translation.

1. 清洁袋
2. 列车广播
3. 乘警
4. 折叠小桌
5. 通告
6. 全体乘务员
7. 代表
8. 终点站
9. 北京铁路局
10. 全天候的
11. 餐车
12. 提前
13. 准时的
14. 共同的
15. 办公场所
16. 身份证
17. 组成的

18. 餐饮供应

Ⅱ. **Sentences translation**

1. 全体乘务员请注意,车站已经开始检票了,请打开车门迎接旅客。

2. 列车启动后,请不要和站台上的亲友握手,以免发生危险。

3. 本次列车为您服务的是哈尔滨铁路的员工,我们将竭诚为您营造一个高效、愉快的氛围。

4. 我们竭诚为旅客提供全天候服务。

5. 我们的工作人员现在将到每节车厢进行查票工作,请各位旅客听到广播后回到您的座位或铺位等待我们工作人员的到来,感谢您的合作。

6. 请您带好所有的行李物品到车厢两端等候下车。

7. 请您按顺序下车,不要拥挤。

8. 为了保持终点站的清洁,列车上的卫生间要提前关闭,请旅客朋友们提前使用。

9. 我谨代表列车全体工作人员感谢您对我们工作的支持与协助。

10. 希望下次旅行再乘坐本次列车,祝愿我们再次相逢。

Unit 13

Getting Off the Train

Section A: Starting Out

Read and match the expressions.

1. crew room
2. power socket
3. undrinkable water
4. China Standard EMU Train
5. equipment and facilities in the carriage
6. have a seating capacity of 80 people
7. offer personal service
8. CRH Train

A. 中国高速铁路
B. 非饮用水
C. 车厢设备设施
D. 定员 80 人
E. 电源插座
F. 中国标准动车组
G. 提供专人服务
H. 乘务室

Section B: Listening and Speaking

SETTING: IN THE CARRIAGE, A PASSENGER IS ASKING FOR INFORMATION. (P = PASSENGER, C = CLERK)

Conversation 1

Activity 1: Listen and answer.

1. What's the next station?

2. Which door could the passenger get off the train?

Activity 2:Listen again and fill in the blanks.

1. Please _____ to get off the train.

2. Which door _____ get off the train?

Activity 3:Work in pairs. Read the conversation at least twice, changing roles each time.

C:Attention, please! The next station is Shanghai. Please get your luggage ready to get off the train.

P:How long will it take to arrive at the station?

C:About 10 minutes. Please check your belongings and don't leave anything on the train.

P:Which door shall we get off the train?

C:The door on the left.

P:I see. Thank you very much.

C:You are welcome.

Activity 4:Please make up your own dialogue with the given information.

A passenger will go to Shanghai, but he doesn't know how long the train will stay at the platform. He is asking something about it in the carriage.

Conversation 2

Activity 1:Listen and answer.

1. When dose the train arrive at Chongqing?

2. Why can't the passenger get the luggage down now?

Activity 2:Listen again and fill in the blanks.

1. Please check your belongings and _____ .

2. _____ , leave it there for a moment.

Activity 3:Work in pairs. Read the conversation at least twice, changing roles each time.

C:Ladies and gentlemen, attention, please! We are arriving at Chongqing in 15 minutes. Please check your belongings and get ready for arrival.

P:Shall I get my luggage down now?

C:I'm afraid you'd better not. For your safety, leave it there for a moment. The train is passing through a tunnel. The light is dim and the train is shaking.

P:Indeed. I can feel it rocking slightly.

C:When the train runs smoothly, I'll help you to get it down.

P:It's very kind of you. Thank you.

C:You are welcome.

Activity 4:Please make up your own dialogue with the given information.

A passenger wants to get off the train and get down his luggage. He is asking something about it in the carriage.

Conversation 3

Activity 1:Listen and answer.

1. Where is the terminal of the train?

2. How does the passenger get the berth ticket back?

Activity 2:Listen again and fill in the blanks.

1. Show me your _____ and you can _____.

2. I'm sorry to say that _____.

Activity 3:Work in pairs. Read the conversation at least twice, changing roles each time.

C :Excuse me, madam. Next stop is our terminal—Beijing Railway Station. Show me your number tally and you can have your berth ticket back. May I tidy up your bedclothes?

P1:Yes, of course. I'm sorry to say that I have stained the bed sheet.

C :Forget it. I'll replace it. I think this watch is yours, isn't it?

P1:Yes, it is mine. Thank you.

C :Don't mention it.

C :(To another passenger) Excuse me, sir. Would you please stand aside? I want to clean the floor.

P2:No problem. Thank you.

C :You are welcome. Whose child is running on the aisle?

P2:Oh, it's my son. He's very excited. This is his first time to take a train.

C :I see. The train is going to stop. Please take care of him.

P2:Yes, I will. Thank you.

Activity 4: Please make up your own dialogue with the given information.

A conductor is going to tidy up the bedclothes in the sleeping car. When the train approaches passenger's destination, the conductor give the passenger the ticket and ask the passenger to return the number tally.

Words and Phrases

get off			下车
arrival	[əˈraɪvl]	n.	到达
shake	[ʃeɪk]	v.	晃动
terminal	[ˈtɜːmɪnl]	n.	终点站
berth ticket			卧铺票
stain	[steɪn]	v.	弄脏
rock	[rɒk]	v.	摇晃
number tally			号码牌

Section C: Passage Reading

Railway Signaling

Railway signaling is a safety system used on railways to prevent trains from colliding. Trains are very susceptible to collision because of running on fixed rails. They are not capable of avoiding a collision by steering away as the vehicles on the road.

In the very early stage of railway development, men were employed to stand next to the line at certain intervals to watch. These men used hand signals to inform train drivers that a preceding train had passed a certain number of minutes ago. This was called "Time Interval Working". If a train had passed the man only a short while ago, the following train was expected to slow down or stop to allow sufficient space between the trains to prevent a collision.

This system was flawed, as the watchman had no way of knowing whether the preceding train had cleared the tracks ahead. If the preceding train broke down or stopped for some reason, the following train would collide with its rear-end. Accidents of this type were common in the early days of railways. However, with the invention of the electrical telegraph, it became possible for the station or signal box ahead to send message back to confirm that a train had passed and that the line ahead was clear. This was called the "Block System".

The Block System came into use gradually during the 1850s and 1860s, and became mandatory in the United Kingdom after parliament passed legislation in 1889 as a response to numerous railway accidents.

Part II/Unit 13 Getting Off the Train

Words and Phrases

signaling	[ˈsɪgnəlɪŋ]	n.	发信号
collide	[kəˈlaɪd]	n.	碰撞
susceptible	[səˈseptəbl]	adj.	易受影响的
interval	[ˈɪntəvl]	n.	间隔
rear-end		n.	后端
mandatory	[ˈmændətəri]	adj.	强制的

Exercises

Ⅰ. Terms translation

1. prevent from
2. be capable of
3. following train
4. slow down
5. break down
6. proceeding train

Ⅱ. Sentences translation

1. Railway signaling is a safety system used on railways to prevent trains from colliding.
2. They are not capable of avoiding a collision by steering away as the vehicles on the road.

Section D: Expanding View

Maglev Train: Flying Without Wings

Maglev train, which uses a technology that uses electromagnets to levitate a train above a guideway, thus eliminating friction, may be a travel solution of the future. For regional travel, it could compete easily with airlines.

The maglev train depends on a principle of magnetism that opposite poles of a magnet attract, like poles repel each other. Instead of running upon a conventional track, the maglev train would run over a guideway lined with electromagnetic coils, some of which designed to levitate and guide the train, others to propel it. The train itself would have large electromagnets on its undercarriage to facilitate levitation and propulsion.

The lack of friction that is inherent in the operation of a maglev train, plus its aerodynamic design, means that such trains can travel in excess of 496km/h, twice as fast as the fastest conventional train, and about 400km/h slower than a Boeing 777. That means a trip between

Boston to Washington would take about 1h and a half. A trip between Houston and Chicago would take just over 3h.

 Words and Phrases ◀◀◀

electromagnet	[ɪˈlektrəʊmægnət]	n.	电磁体
levitate	[ˈlevɪteɪt]	v.	轻轻浮起
guideway	[ˈgaɪdweɪ]	n.	导轨
Maglev Train		n.	磁悬浮列车
eliminate	[ɪˈlɪmɪneɪt]	v.	消除
friction	[ˈfrɪkʃn]	n.	摩擦

 Section E: Self-evaluation

I. Words and phrases translation

1. 行李
2. 下车
3. 终点站
4. 到达
5. 卧铺票
6. 发信号
7. 碰撞
8. 后端
9. 防止
10. 能够
11. 后行列车
12. 先行列车
13. 减慢

14. 出故障

15. 磁悬浮列车

Ⅱ. Sentences translation

1. 请带好您的行李准备下车。

2. 还要多长时间到站?

3. 请检查一下,不要把东西丢在车上。

4. 请问从哪边门下车?

5. 为了您的安全,暂时放一会儿。

6. 等火车行驶平稳后,我再帮您把行李拿下来。

7. 火车就要到达终点站了,我可以整理您的床铺吗?

8. 火车快到站了,请照顾好您的孩子。

Part III

Other Services（其他服务）

Unit 14

Special Passenger Service

Section A: Starting Out

Look at the following signs and pictures of railway transportation and try to guess what they are.

Accessible Elevator	Accessible Toilet	Wheelchair
Accessible Carriage	Accessible Ticket Window	Nursing Room
Baby Care Station	Waiting Room for Special Passengers	

1. _____   2. _____

3. _____   4. _____

5. _____

6. _____

7. _____

8. _____

Section B: Listening and Speaking

SETTING: A PASSENGER IS ASKING FOR INFORMATION ABOUT HOW TO RESERVE THE SPECIAL PASSENGER SERVICE. (P = PASSENGER, C = CLERK)

Conversation 1

Activity 1: Listen and answer.

1. How to make a Special Passenger Service Reservations?
2. Why does the passengers need to reserve Special Passenger Service?

Activity 2: Listen again and fill in the blanks.

1. How can I _____ the Special Passenger Service?
2. You can dial the _____ to reserve it.

112

Activity 3: Work in pairs. Read the conversation at least twice, changing roles each time.

C: Good morning! Can I help you?

P: Good morning! Do you know how to reserve the Special Passenger Service?

C: You can log on the website (Railway Customer Service Center of China): www.12306.com and fill in a form, or you can dial the Railway Hotline 12306 to reserve it.

P: Thank you. My grandfather has trouble in walking, so he needs extra help to get on and off the train.

C: It is a good choice to reserve the Special Passenger Service.

P: I think so. Thank you.

C: You are welcome.

Activity 4: Please make up your own dialogue based on the fallowing situation.

A sick passenger needs to reserve the Special Passenger Service. His friend will dial the Railway Hotline 12306 to reserve it. Suppose you are a clerk, you will answer the passenger's questions and ask the information of passenger to complete the process of reservation.

Conversation 2

SETTING: A PASSENGER IS ASKING FOR INFORMATION ABOUT ACCESSIBLE TOILET ONTHE TRAIN.

Activity 1: Listen and answer.

1. Is there any accessible toilet on this train?
2. How to flush the toilet?

Activity 2: Listen again and fill in the blanks.

1. How can I get to the _____?
2. This toilet is equipped with a handrail and _____.

Activity 3: Work in pairs. Read the conversation at least twice, changing roles each time.

P: Excuse me. Is there any accessible toilet on this train?

C: Yes. There is only one in Carriage 4 of this train. This toilet is equipped with a handrail and emergency call button.

P: How can I get to the accessible toilet?

C: Please follow me. Keep going ahead then you can see it at the other end of the

```
   Carriage 4.
     P:Thank you. (3min later…)
     C:It's occupied. Please wait.
     P:OK, by the way, how to flush the toilet?
     C:The flush button is on the wall. Please press it after using the toilet. And you can use
   the sensor tap to wash your hands.
     P:Thank you very much.
```

Activity 4:Please make up your own dialogue based on the fallowing situations.

A passenger knocks over a cup of water carelessly and got her baby's clothes wet on the train. She needs to change the dry clothes for her baby, but she doesn't know where she can do it. She is asking the clerk about the information.

Conversation 3

SETTING: AN ELDERLY PASSENGER IS GETTING A TRAIN SICKNESS. SHE IS ASKING A CLERK FOR HELP.

Activity 1:Listen and answer.

1. What's wrong with the elderly passenger?

2. How did the clerk deal with it?

Activity 2:Listen again and fill in the blanks.

1. I don't feel very well. I think I get a little bit _____.

2. We have some medicines for a train sickness in _____.

Activity 3: Work in pairs. Read the conversation at least twice, changing roles each time.

```
     P:Excuse me.
     C:Yes. What can I do for you?
     P:I don't feel very well. I think I get a little bit train sickness.
     C:Oh, I'm sorry to hear that. What's the matter with you?
     P:I feel dizzy and I want to vomit. Do you have medicines for a train sickness?
     C:Take it easy. Here is the vomit bag. We have some medicines for train sickness in the
   first aid box. Just a moment, please. I will get it for you.
```

Part III/Unit 14　Special Passenger Service

P: Thank you. (3min later…)
C: Here are the medicines and a cup of water. Take it, please. You will feel better soon.
P: Thank you very much.
C: You are welcome.

Activity 4: Please make up your own dialogue based on the fallowing situation.

A woman looks rather pale and suddenly fainted on the train. Suppose you are a clerk, you will deal with this emergency case and make the first aid.

Words and Phrases

reserve	[rɪˈzɜːv]	v.	预定
Special Passenger Service			特殊旅客服务
Railway Hotline			铁路客服电话
accessible toilet			无障碍厕所
Emergency Call Button			紧急按钮
sensor tap			感应水龙头
vomit	[ˈvɒmɪt]		呕吐
dial	[ˈdaɪəl]	v.	拨打
Railway Customer Service Center of China			中国铁路客户服务中心
handrail	[ˈhændreɪl]	n.	扶手
flush	[flʌʃ]	v.	冲
train sickness			晕车
dizzy	[ˈdɪzi]	adj.	头晕
first aid box			急救箱

Section C: Passage Reading

The special passengers including the elderly, young, sick, disabled, pregnant, and the people with mobility difficulties can make a reservation in the following ways:

▶ Logging on the Railway Customer Service Center Website: www.12306.cn.
▶ Logging on "Shanghai Railway 12306" App.
▶ Going to the Service Counter of railway station.
▶ Dialing Railway Hotline 12306.

When you make a reservation, please provide the following information: departure time, train number, number of special passenger, contact information, and so on. When we (Railway Sectors) get your requirement, we will do our best to provide you with quality service, including: offering wheelchair and stretcher, giving priority to entering and exiting the station in advance, assisting in taking the elevator.

 ## Words and Phrases

disabled	[dɪsˈeɪbld]	adj.	残疾的
mobility	[məʊˈbɪlətɪ]	n.	移动性
log on			登录
quality service			优质服务
stretcher	[ˈstretʃə(r)]	n.	担架
assist	[əˈsɪst]	v.	协助
pregnant	[ˈpregnənt]	adj.	怀孕的
make a reservation			预定
departure time			发车时间
wheelchair	[ˈwiːltʃeə(r)]	n.	轮椅
in advance			提前
elevator	[ˈelɪveɪtə(r)]	n.	升降电梯

 ## Exercises

Ⅰ. Terms translation

1. make a reservation
2. departure time
3. quality service
4. in advance

Ⅱ. Sentences translation

1. Logging on "Shanghai Railway 12306" App.
2. Going to the Service Counter of railway station.
3. Please provide the following information: departure time, train number, number of special passenger, contact information, and so on.
4. We will do our best to provide you with quality service.

 Section D: Expanding View

Shanghai Maglev Train

Shanghai Maglev Train (Shanghai Transrapid)(上海磁悬浮示范运营线) is the first commercial high-speed maglev line in the world. Construction of the line began in March, 2002, and the trial service commenced on January 1st, 2004.

The line is operated by Shanghai Maglev Transportation Development Co., Ltd.. The project took 10 billion RMB and 2.5 years. The train runs from Longyang Road station on the Shanghai Subway Line 2 to Pudong International Airport, and the total track length is about 30km.

The train can reach the speed of 350km/h in 2min, with a maximum speed of 431km/h. The train takes 7min and 20s to complete the journey.

The maglev train has a length of 153m, a width of 3.7m, a height of 4.2m and 3 seat levels. And it has a passenger capacity of 874 persons. The departure interval is 15min.

Words and Phrases ◄◄◄

maglev	['mæglev]	n.	磁悬浮
commercial	[kə'mɜːʃl]	adj.	商业的
a maximum speed			最大时速
trail service			试运行
commence	[kə'mens]	v.	开始;着手
Passenger capacity			载客量

Section E: Self-evaluation

I. Words and phrases translation

1. 无障碍电梯
2. 无障碍厕所
3. 婴儿护理台
4. 重点旅客候车室
5. 轮椅

6. 预约重点旅客服务

7. 铁路客服电话

8. 晕车(火车)

9. 扶手

10. 紧急呼叫按钮

11. 感应水龙头

12. 试运行

13. 最大时速

14. 载客量

Ⅱ. Sentences translation

1. 你知道如何预约重点旅客服务吗?

2. 你可以登录网站:www.12306.com,或者拨打铁路客服12306办理。

3. 请问怎么去无障碍厕所?

4. 冲水按钮在墙上,请按压按钮。另外,你可以使用感应式水龙头洗手。

5. 我觉得不舒服,我有点晕车。

6. 您哪儿不舒服呢?

7. 我们有晕车的药,在急救箱里。稍等会,我去给您拿。

8. 上海磁悬浮示范运营线是世界上第一条高速磁悬浮铁路商业运行线。

9. 在轨运营里程近30千米。

Part III/Unit 15 Complaints

Unit 15

Complaints

 Section A: Starting Out

Look at the following signs of complaint channels and try to guess what they are.

Inquiry Office/Information Office	News media
Hotline operator	Letters

1. _____

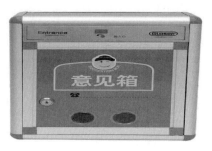

2. _____

3. _____

4. _____

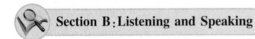

Section B: Listening and Speaking

SETTING: AT THE INFORMATION/INQUIRY OFFICE A PASSENGER IS ASKING FOR INFORMATION. (P = PASSENGER, C = CLERK)

Conversation 1

Activity 1: Listen and answer.

1. Why the toilet is locked?
2. How long will the train stop at this station?

Activity 2: Listen again and fill in the blanks.

1. Toilet on the train _____ used when it stops at stations.
2. You have to _____. Sorry for the _____.

Activity 3: Work in pairs. Read the conversation at least twice, changing roles each time.

P: Is the toilet occupied?
C: No, it is locked.
P: Why?
C: Because the train is approaching the station. Toilets on the train are not supposed to be used when it stops at stations.
P: Oh, I see. How long will the train stop at this station?
C: 5min. You have to wait for a while. Sorry for the inconvenience.
P: I see. Thank you!
C: You're welcome.

Activity 4: Please make up your own dialogue with the given information.

Equipment failure, passengers can't get through the gate.

Conversation 2

Activity 1: Listen and answer.

1. Why are there no trains in sight?

2. How long will it take for the train to arrive?

Activity 2: Listen again and fill in the blanks.

1. Sorry, _____ knocked out service on the line 10min ago.

2. The power was resumed _____, but it may _____ 25min for the train to arrive.

Activity 3: Work in pairs. Read the conversation at least twice, changing roles each time.

P: What's up? The station is thronged with passengers, but not a single train is in sight.
C: Sorry, great capacity knocked out service on the line 10 minutes ago.
P: How long will it take to restore the power?
C: The power was resumed just a moment ago, but it may take about 25 minutes for the train to arrive.
P: Oh, that's too long. I can't wait. What should I do with my ticket?
C: You can get a refund at the Service Center.
P: I see.
C: Goodbye, and sorry again for the inconvenience.

Activity 4: Please make up your own dialogue based on the fallowing situation.

A passenger is smoking in the carriage. A clerk is trying to persuade him not to smoke.

Conversation 3

Activity 1: Listen and answer.

1. What does the passenger complain about?

2. To what extent is the passenger's certificate damaged?

Activity 2: Listen again and fill in the blanks.

1. The pages in it _____ the cover and somewhat old, but the characters are still _____.

2. You are allowed to go in through _____ as long as your certificate is in order and can be _____.

Activity 3: Work in pairs. Read the conversation at least twice, changing roles each time.

P: Excuse me! I am here to complain that the staff of your station is not very responsible.
C: Oh, I am sorry for that. Can you tell me in detail?

P: Though several pages inside my certificate were damaged, it was still very easy for the staff to recognize my identification. However, the staff didn't allow me to enter station through the side door. I had to buy a ticket of 5 yuan to go in.

C: Oh, to what extent is your certificate damaged?

P: The pages in it are separated from the cover and somewhat old, but the characters are still clear enough to read.

C: Then did the staff tell you in what condition he would allow you to go in through the side door?

P: After checking my certificate, he just said, "You can't go in through the side door and you have to buy a ticket."

C: You are allowed to go in through the side door as long as your certificate is in order and can be recognized easily. We will educate the staff concerned and improve our service. We apologize for any inconvenience this might cause.

Activity 4: Please make up your own dialogue based on the fallowing situation.
A passenger is now complaining about great capacity.

Words and Phrases

characters	[ˈkærəktəz]	n.	特性；[计]字符
situation	[ˌsɪtjʊˈeɪʃn]	n.	情况；处境
capacity	[kəˈpæsɪtɪ]	n.	容量
Service Center			服务中心
inconvenience	[ˌɪnkənˈviːnɪəns]	n.	不便；麻烦
identification	[aɪˌdentɪfɪˈkeɪʃn]	n.	身份证明
concerned	[kənˈsɜːnd]	adj.	有关的
similar	[ˈsɪmɪlə]	adj.	相似的

Section C: Passage Reading

Usually, a complaint processing has to go through four stages. They are complaint acceptance, investigation, resolution and service improvement. Complaint acceptance refers to the collecting and collating process of content and detailed information about passenger's dissatisfaction and claims. Only through the investigation of the truth and clear distinction can complaints be handled justly. Complaint resolution includes two parts. One is to respond to the passenger in question after investigation. Another is to develop a more effective solution until the passenger in question is satisfied. The core goal of continuous improvement is to improve the quality of service products and effectiveness of handling complaints.

Words and Phrases

acceptance	[əkˈseptəns]	n.	接纳
resolution	[ˌrezəˈluːʃn]	n.	解决
effective	[ɪˈfektɪv]	adj.	有效的
investigation	[ɪnˌvestɪˈgeɪʃn]	n.	调查
refer to			关于
distinction	[dɪˈstɪŋkʃn]	n.	区别

Exercises

I. Terms translation

1. in what condition
2. knock out
3. respond to
4. be satisfied
5. the core goal of

II. Sentence translation

1. Toilet on the train are not supposed to be used when it stops at station.

2. The station is thronged with passengers, but not a single train is in sight.

3. You are allowed to go in through the side door as long as your certificate is in order and can be recognized easily.

4. Only through the investigation of the truth and clear distinction can complaints be handled justly.

Section D: Expanding View

Monorail

A monorail is a railway in which the track consists of a single rail. The term is also used to describe the beam of the system, or the trains traveling on such a beam or track. The term originates from joining "mono (one)" and "rail (rail)".

Monorails have found applications in airport transfer and medium capacity metros. To differentiate monorails from other transport modes, the Monorail Society defines a monorail as a "single rail serving as a track for passengers or freight vehicles." In most cases rail is elevated, but monorails can also run at grade, below grade, or in subway tunnels. Vehicles either are suspended from or straddle a narrow guide way. Monorail vehicles are wider than the guide way that supports them.

Monorail vehicles often appear similar to light rail vehicles, and can be manned or unmanned. They can be individual rigid vehicle, articulated single unit, or multiple units coupled into trains. Like other advanced rapid transit systems, monorails can be driven by linear induction motors; like conventional railways, the vehicle bodies can be connected to the beam via bogies, allowing curves to be negotiated.

Words and Phrases

medium	[ˈmiːdɪəm]	adj.	中等的
originate	[əˈrɪdʒɪneɪt]	v.	发源
vehicle	[ˈviːɪkl]	n.	交通工具
straddle	[ˈstrædl]	v.	跨立于
manned	[mænd]	adj.	有人驾驶的
multiple	[ˈmʌltɪpl]	adj.	许多的
beam	[biːm]	n.	横梁
differentiate	[ˌdɪfəˈrenʃɪeɪt]	v.	区别
suspend	[səˈspend]	v.	使悬浮
narrow	[ˈnærəʊ]	adj.	狭窄的
articulated	[ɑːˈtɪkjʊleɪtɪd]	adj.	铰接式的

Section E: Self-evaluation

I. Words and phrases translation

1. 折扣票
2. 检票口
3. 押金
4. 学生票

5. 敬老票

6. 换乘

7. 客服中心

8. 优先座

9. 怀孕妇女

10. 消防通道

Ⅱ. Sentences translation

1. 请问为什么自动售票机无法出票？

2. 今天车厢内的空调效果非常不好，感觉很冷。

3. 安检处的工作人员不太认真，在乘客行李过安检时玩手机。

4. 为什么我的储值票显示为无效票？

5. 站内卫生间打扫不干净，严重影响乘客使用体验。

Unit 16

Lost and Found

Section A: Starting Out

Look at the following signs of railway transportation and try to guess what they are.

```
Phone              ID Cards
Key                Lost and Found Office
```

1. _____

2. _____

3. _____

4. _____

Section B:Listening and Speaking

SETTING:AT THE INFORMATION/ENQUIRY OFFICE, A PASSENGER IS ASKING FOR INFORMATION. (P = PASSENGER, C = CLERK)

Conversation 1

Activity 1:Listen and answer.

1. What did the passenger lose?
2. Where should the passenger go to get his umbrella back?

Activity 2:Listen again and fill in the blanks.

1. I left my umbrella here, now it _____ .
2. It's now kept at the _____ .

Activity 3:Work in pairs. Read the conversation at least twice, changing roles each time.

C:Good morning. Can I help you?
P:I left my umbrella here, now it has gone.
C:I was told someone had picked up an umbrella. It's now kept at the service counter. You'd better go and see if it is yours.
P:Oh, it's very nice of you.

Activity 4:Please make up your own dialogue with the given information.

Peter lost a rectangular black briefcase this morning at about 11 o'clock at Guangzhou South Railway Station.

Conversation 2

Activity 1:Listen and answer.

1. Where was the passenger from?
2. Did the passenger find her bag?

Activity 2:Listen again and fill in the blanks.

1. I have just left _____ on the train when I got off. I am here to _____ .

2. Could you give a description of your lost bag _____?

Activity 3:Work in pairs. Read the conversation at least twice, changing roles each time.

C:Good morning, Lost and Found Office. What can I do for you?

P:Good morning, I am Chen Mei from Chengdu. I have just left my handbag on the train when I got off. I am here to claim it.

C:Could you give a description of your lost bag as detailed as possible?

P:A red leather handbag.

C:Can I see your identification?

P:Sure, here is my ID Card.

C:Could you fill in this request form?

P:OK.

S:Here is your handbag. A passenger found it on the train.

P:How kind he is! Thank you.

Activity 4:Please make up your own dialogue based on the fallowing situation.

Susan left her key case at the waiting room. There is a set of keys in the case and it has a pink dolphin ornament.

Conversation 3

Activity 1:Listen and answer.

1. Where did the passenger go after the last time he used his phone or saw it?

2. What is the model and color of the passenger's phone?

Activity 2:Listen again and fill in the blanks.

1. I have got a call from _____ when I just arrived at _____.

2. And your contact number. We'll inform you when we _____.

Activity 3:Work in pairs. Read the conversation at least twice, changing roles each time.

C:Good afternoon, sir. What can I do for you?

P:I have just lost my phone, there are very important contact numbers in it.

C:Do you remember the last time you used it or saw it, and where was it?

P:I have got a call from my wife when I just arrived at the entrance.

C:Where did you go after that?

P: I took the ticket and went to the waiting hall.
C: What's your phone number? Has the phone been connected yet?
P: No, the phone was shut down.
C: What is the model of your phone? And what's the color?
P: It's a white iPhone 8.
C: May I have your name, and your ID Card?
P: OK, my name is Li Ming. Here is my certificate.
C: And your contact number. We'll inform you when we get a trace of it.
P: Thank you.
C: You are welcome.

Activity 4: Please make up your own dialogue based on the fallowing situation.

A passenger has lost her wedding ring. It's a round gold ring with a beautiful crystal rose on it.

Words and Phrases

rectangular	[rekˈtæŋgjələ(r)]	adj.	矩形的;成直角的
briefcase	[ˈbriːfkeɪs]	n.	公文包
description	[dɪˈskrɪpʃn]	n.	描述;描写
ornament	[ˈɔːnəmənt]	n.	装饰物
waiting hall			候车室
claim	[kleɪm]	v.	声称;主张;认领
trace	[treɪs]	n.	踪迹
form	[fɔːm]	n.	表格

Section C: Passage Reading

Leaders of Beijing's oldest Subway Line 1 said that they had picked up about 8200 lost items during the past 5 years, especially on the 4 largest stations which are Tian'anmen East, Wangfujing, Dongdan, Tian'anmen West. It was increasing year by year.

According to statistics, in 2007, metro stations picked up about 1200 lost items altogether, and in 2011 it was about 2000.

The relevant metro service tries to remind passengers of intensifying consciousness to take good care of their belongings, not to forget or lose things, such as the ticket. If passengers have lost something, contact with the staff as soon as possible. If the items have been left behind in the train, compartment numbers or travel times should be provided. If the items have been left behind in orbit, please inform the staff and not jump off to pick up yourself.

 Words and Phrases ◀◀◀

pick up			捡起;获得
statistics	[stə'tɪstɪks]	n.	统计
consciousness	['kɒnʃəsnəs]	n.	意识;知觉
intensifying	[ɪn'tensɪfaɪɪŋ]	v.	(使)增强;加剧
compartment	[kəm'pɑːtmənt]	n.	隔间
jump off			跳下;开始行动
especially	[ɪ'speʃəli]	adv.	特别;尤其
property	['prɒpəti]	n.	财产;性质
belonging	[bɪ'lɒŋɪŋ]	n.	所有物;行李
leave behind			留下;遗留
orbit	['ɔːbɪt]	n.	轨道

 Exercises

Ⅰ. Terms translation

1. Service Counter
2. Lost and Found Office
3. as detailed as possible
4. shut down
5. according to statistics
6. with all-out effort
7. to resume operation
8. property loss
9. take good care of
10. window seat

Ⅱ. Sentence translation

1. What have you got inside?
2. Don't worry. We'll manage to give it back to you if we find it.
3. We'll keep you informed.
4. Please take your belongings with you.
5. Sorry, your luggage is overweight. Please buy a luggage ticket.

Section D: Expanding View

China train stations

China has over 5500 railway stations for passenger use along its 127000km long rail lines.

The early-built China train stations are usually located in the center of the city or town, operating non-bullet trains and some also operating a few bullet ones. The newly-built railway stations are generally located far from the city center and specialized in high-speed trains, such as Beijing South, Shanghai Hongqiao and Xi'an North; but they mostly can be reached by metro.

A train station in China usually consists of one or two squares, and a terminal building, inside which ticket offices, waiting rooms, boarding gates, platforms and some affiliated facilities like toilets, hot drinking water, restaurants and bilingual direction boards are provided.

Words and Phrases

specialized	[ˈspeʃəlaɪzd]	adj.	专业的
affiliated	[əˈfɪlɪeɪtɪd]	adj.	附属的
bilingual	[baɪˈlɪŋgwəl]	adj.	双语的
facility	[fəˈsɪləti]	n.	设施、设备
consist of			组成

 Section E: Self-evaluation

I. Words and phrases translation

1. 候机楼
2. 行李寄存处

3. 母婴候车室

4. 方向箭头

5. 自动售票机

6. 儿童票

7. 驾驶车厢

8. 餐车

9. 广播室

10. 残疾人卫生间

Ⅱ. Sentences translation

1. 请保持过道畅通。

2. 您的行李可以放在这里(大件行李处),贵重物品请随身携带。

3. 乘车时,不要随意扳动或按下车上的紧急制动阀。

4. 靠背可以调整得舒服些,按钮在这里。

Part III/Unit 17　Emergency Response

Unit 17

Emergency Response

Section A: Starting Out

Look at the following signs and try to guess what they are.

```
emergency call button            fire extinguisher
emergency door handle inside     emergency hammer
```

1. _____

2. _____

3. _____

4. _____

 Section B:Listening and Speaking

SETTING:AT THE INFORMATION/ENQUIRY OFFICE, A PASSENGER IS ASKING FOR INFORMATION. (P = PASSENGER, C = CLERK)

Conversation 1

Activity 1:Listen and answer.

1. Is there any emergency?

2. Why dose the train cannot move on?

Activity 2:Listen again and fill in the blanks.

1. Dear passengers, the train cannot move on due to _____.

2. Train staff shall start _____ immediately and carry out emergence response _____ the established procedure.

Activity 3: Work in pairs. Read the conversation at least twice, changing roles each time.

P:Excuse me. Is there any emergency?

C:I am sorry. This is a temporary stop now.

P:Why? I am a little nervous.

C:We apologize to you for any inconvenience. But clam down, please. I don't know the reason for the delay. We'll inform you as soon as possible.

P:Bad luck.

C:(After 2min). Dear passengers, the train cannot move on due to the signal system problem. On behalf of the railway staff, I make an apology to all of you sincerely. Thank you for your cooperation.

P:What should we do if the emergency happens?

C:In case of the train delay, temporary power failure, air-conditioning failure, fire, explosion or other emergencies, please keep calm, follow the instruction of the train staff and maintain good order. Train staff shall start emergency plans immediately and carry out emergence response in accordance with the established procedure. But I believe that the problem will be solved soon.

P:I hope so!

C:Thank you for your cooperation.

Activity 4: Please make up your own dialogue with the given information.

The train is making a temporary stop for the temporary power failure. A passenger is asking something about it in the carriage.

Conversation 2

Activity 1: Listen and answer.

1. What is the matter with the passenger?
2. What does the clerk do finally?

Activity 2: Listen again and fill in the blanks.

1. Excuse me. Could you _____?

2. I am having a fever but I feel a little cold, could you _____ the air conditioner?

Activity 3: Work in pairs. Read the conversation at least twice, changing roles each time.

P: Excuse me. Could you do me a favor?
C: Of course. What can I do for you?
P: I am having a fever but I feel a little cold, could you turn down the air conditioner?
C: I am sorry, it is summer and it is very hot outside the carriage. If I turned down the air conditioner, the other passenger would feel hot. But I can get you a blanket, is that all right?
P: That's OK. Thank you.
C: I will be right back.

Activity 4: Please make up your own dialogue based on the fallowing situation.

A passenger was having fever on the train, and he is asking help for the clerk.

Conversation 3

Activity 1: Listen and answer.

1. What's the matter with the passenger?
2. How does the clerk help the passenger?

Activity 2:Listen again and fill in the blanks.

1. I can help you find your daughter by _____.

2. Please write down the girl's name, age—_____.

Activity 3:Work in pairs. Read the conversation at least twice, changing roles each time.

P:Excuse me. Could you do me a favor?

C:What is the matter with you?

P:I can't find my daughter. I'm so concerned for her safety.

C:Please don't worry. I can help you find your daughter by broadcasting an announcement. Please write down the girl's name, age, your name and your carriage number. By the way, what are the characteristics of your daughter?

P:OK. She is 6 years old, wearing a white dress. Let me write down the information on the paper.

C:Madam, I'll make an announcement to look for your child. I will inform you as soon as possible.

P:Thank you.

C:(a moment later.) Ladies and gentlemen, may I have your attention, please? A six-year-old girl was lost from her family. The girl from America wears a white dress. Her mother is waiting for her in Car 2.

P:Thank you very much.

C:You are welcome. I believe we will find her soon.

Activity 4:Please make up your own dialogue with the given information.

A passenger on the train cannot find his son. He is asking the clerk for help.

 Words and Phrases ◂◂◂

emergency	[ɪˈmɜːdʒənsɪ]	n.	紧急情况
temporary	[ˈtemprərɪ]	adj.	临时的
apologize	[əˈpɒlədʒaɪz]	v.	道歉
inconvenience	[ˌɪnkənˈviːnɪəns]	n.	不方便
clam down			冷静
in accordance with			根据;与……一致
power failure			停电
instruction	[ɪnˈstrʌkʃn]	n.	指令
maintain	[meɪnˈteɪn]	v.	保持
procedure	[prəˈsiːdʒə(r)]	n.	程序
blanket	[ˈblæŋkɪt]	n.	毛毯

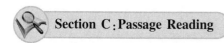 Section C: Passage Reading

International Train Ticket

Purchase an International Train Ticket

Passengers could purchase international train tickets at the railway station directly. However, it is always difficult for passengers to buy tickets on the spot since the tickets are needed urgently. So, it is suggested that passengers book tickets through travel agencies that are commissioned to sell international train tickets. The travel agencies may charge relevant service fee.

International train tickets can be booked through travel agencies 40 days in advance. A deposit is required for pre-booking but this will be returned to you when you buy your ticket. After pre-booking, passengers should pay for their tickets in full at least 7 days ahead of the trains' departure date. Otherwise, the booking will be canceled automatically and the booking fee will not be returned. A valid passport and visa to the destination country are required to be presented when buying an international ticket.

Return an International Train Ticket

The return of tickets can be handled by yourself at the railway stations.

If an international train ticket is returned 72h ahead of the scheduled departure time, 80% of the fare will be refund. No service charge is refund.

If an international train ticket is returned or changed less than 72h ahead of the scheduled departure time, 80% of the seat-ticket fare or 20% of the sleeper fare will be refund. No service charge is refund.

If an international train ticket is returned or changed less than 3h after the train leaving, 80% of a seat-ticket fare will be refund but no fare will be refund for a sleeper-ticket. No service charge is refund.

Please note the return of tickets may not be allowed if you book the tickets through an agency. You'd better confirm the regulations of the specific agency before booking.

 Words and Phrases ◀◀◀

purchase	[ˈpɜːtʃəs]	v.	购买
urgently	[ˈɜːdʒəntlɪ]	adv.	急迫的
commission	[kəˈmɪʃn]	v.	授予
relevant	[ˈreləvənt]	adj.	相关的
deposit	[dɪˈpɒzɪt]	n.	存款
cancel	[ˈkænsl]	v.	取消

passport	[ˈpɑːspɔːt]	n.	护照
visa	[ˈviːzə]	n.	签证
present	[ˈpreznt]	v.	提交；显示
refund	[ˈriːfʌnd]	n.	资金偿还；退还

Exercises

I. Terms translation

1. travel agency
2. in advance
3. scheduled departure time
4. service

II. Sentence translation

1. So, it is suggested that passengers book tickets through travel agencies that are commissioned to sell international train tickets.
2. International train tickets can be booked through travel agencies 40 days in advance.
3. You'd better confirm the regulations of the specific agency before booking.

Section D: Expanding View

The Spring Festival Travel Rush

The Spring Festival Travel Rush is also known as the Chinese New Year Travel Rush, the Lunar New Year Travel Rush, or Chunyun in China. It usually begins 15 days ahead of the Chinese New Year and 25 days after, lasting for 40 days. During the Spring Festival Travel Rush, China's transportation system, especially its railway system, faces an extremely heavy traffic load, which results in great difficulties in obtaining tickets, crowded railway stations and train carriages, etc. About 357 million passenger trips were made during China's 2017 Spring Festival Travel Rush. It is no doubt that Chunyun becomes the largest annual human migration on earth.

Millions of people working or studying out of their hometowns will be hurrying home to reunite with their families as the Chinese New Year approaches. This long held tradition is the main reason for the travel rush. Another reason is that the holiday is one of the two week long holidays of the year, therefore it becomes the perfect travel time for many people.

The 40 days of Chunyun period imposes great challenges on the inter-city transportation system. The demand for tickets far exceeds the supply. Various measures such as adding many temporary trains, extending the working hours of the booking office and opening up more booths have been adopted to alleviate this problem. The real-name system is taken to relieve the difficulty in buying tickets and effectively stop scalpers who profit a lot during this period. Another problem is the disorder and insecurity brought by more people crowding train stations or carriages. Therefore more police officers are deployed to maintain the public security.

 Words and Phrases

rush	[rʌʃ]	n.	匆忙
annual	[ˈænjʊəl]	adj.	每年的
migration	[maɪˈgreɪʃn]	n.	迁徙
reunite	[ˌriːjuːˈnaɪt]	v.	重聚
tradition	[trəˈdɪʃn]	n.	传统
exceed	[ɪkˈsiːd]	v.	超越
traffic load			交通压力
maintain the public security			维护公共安全
temporary	[ˈtemprərɪ]	adj.	临时的
alleviate	[əˈliːvɪeɪt]	v.	减轻
relieve	[rɪˈliːv]	v.	缓解
scalper	[ˈskælpə(r)]		(门票等的)倒卖者
deploy	[dɪˈplɔɪ]		部署;调度
Spring Festival Travel Rush			春节出游高峰
real-name system			实名制

 Section E: Self-evaluation

Ⅰ. Words and phrases translation

1. 应急锤
2. 紧急呼叫按钮
3. 灭火器
4. 紧急开门阀

5. 临时的

6. 停电

7. 指令

8. 毛毯

9. 购买

10. 取消

11. 护照

12. 签证

13. 旅行社

14. 春运

15. 实名制

Ⅱ. Sentences translation

1. 现在是临时停车。

2. 请镇定,我不知道耽误的原因。

3. 如有发送列车晚点、临时停电、空调故障、火灾、爆炸或其他紧急情况,请保持冷静,听从列车工作人员的指挥,保持良好的秩序。

4. 请问能帮我一个忙吗?

5. 可以把空调温度调低一点吗?

6. 我很担心她的安全。

7. 我可以通过广播帮您找孩子。

8. 您的孩子有什么特征?

9. 请问有紧急情况吗?

10. 我相信很快就会收到好消息的。

Part III/Unit 18 Thanks, Apologies and Advice

Unit 18

Thanks, Apologies and Advice

 Section A: Starting Out

Look at the following signs and try to guess what they are.

Ticket barrier	Please Conserve Water	Self-service Ticket Office
No Littering	Please Do Not Touch	No Spitting

1. _____

2. _____

3. _____

4. _____

5. _____   6. _____

Section B: Listening and Speaking

SETTING: A PASSENGER IS ASKING FOR INFORMATION. (P = PASSENGER , C = CREW)

Conversation 1

Activity 1: Listen and answer.

1. What's the difference between the first-class seat and second-class seat?
2. Why the passenger can't get in the VIP section?

Activity 2: Listen again and fill in the blanks.

1. It is _____ and _____ , and offers a personal service. Besides, you _____ .

2. This is the VIP section _____ And the seats are not for _____ .

Activity 3: Work in pairs. Read the conversation at least twice, changing roles each time.

P: How is a VIP seat better than a first-Class seat?

C: It is quieter and more comfortable, and offers a personal service. Besides, you can look into the driver's cabin.

P: What's the difference between the first-class and second-class seats?

C: A first-class seat has more space and is more comfortable. Besides, it is equipped with a video player.

P: What's this carriage over here?

C: This is the VIP section in the front of the train. And the seats are not for passengers.

Part III/Unit 18 Thanks, Apologies and Advice

P: May I get in and have a look?

C: I'm sorry. For safety reasons, passengers are not allowed to take pictures or look around. Otherwise, they might distract the driver's attention.

P: OK. I see.

C: Thank you for your cooperation.

Activity 4: Please make up your own dialogue with the given information.

A passenger is interested in the speed of the high-speed train. Please tell him some relevant information. Maybe you can use the following words: fast, the highest speed, 350km/h and electronic screen.

Conversation 2

Activity 1: Listen and answer.

1. What souvenirs do the people who come here usually buy?

2. What souvenirs are the passenger going to buy?

Activity 2: Listen again and fill in the blanks.

1. Anything else? Are there anything for _____ and _____?

2. They are Chinese brush, _____, _____ and Xuan _____.

Activity 3: Work in pairs. Read the conversation at least twice, changing roles each time.

P: Excuse me?

C: What can I do for you, sir?

P: I want to get some souvenirs for myself. Could you give me some advice?

C: OK. Many people arrive here will buy silk, fan or Dragon Well Tea.

P: Anything else? Are there anything for Calligraphy and Paintings?

C: Maybe "The Scholar's Four Jewels" are more suitable for you.

P: What are they?

C: They are Chinese brush, black ink, ink stone and Xuan paper.

P: Thank you very much. I'll get them. It's very kind of you.

C: My pleasure. Hope you a good journey.

Activity 4:Please make up your own dialogue based on the fallowing situation.

A passenger wants you to introduce him the Sichuan cuisine. You may use the following words:world-famous, hot and spicy flavors, recommend, specialties, bean curd with mince and chilli oil, pork shreds with fishy flavor, translucent beef slices.

Conversation 3

Activity 1:Listen and answer.

1. What did this passenger lose?
2. Can the crew accept gifts from passengers?

Activity 2:Listen again and fill in the blanks.

1. Your service is very _____ and _____.
2. Thank you for your _____. We are just doing our job.

Activity 3:Work in pairs. Read the conversation at least twice, changing roles each time.

P:I will leave the train. I have a wonderful time during this trip. Thank you for everything you have done for me.

C:Don't mention it. It's very nice to have you on our trip.

P:Without your timely help, I couldn't have regained my lost bag.

C:I'm very glad I can do something for you.

P:Your service is very thoughtful and satisfactory. Here's a gift for you.

C:Thank you for your compliment. We are just doing our job. But it is our rule that we do not accept gifts from passengers. But thanks all the same. Thank you for coming. See you next time.

P:See you.

Activity 4:Please make up your own dialogue based on the fallowing situation.

Suppose you are a passenger. You lost your bag during the journey. The car attendant helped you and found it. Make up a dialogue with your partner.

 Words and Phrases

ticket barrier			检票口
cabin	[ˈkæbɪn]	n.	舱
section	[ˈsekʃn]	n.	部门

Dragon Well Tea			龙井茶
painting	[ˈpeɪntɪŋ]	n.	绘画
Chinese brush			毛笔
ink-stone			砚台
regain	[rɪˈgeɪn]	v.	复得
equip	[ɪˈkwɪp]	v.	配备
distract	[dɪˈstrækt]	v.	使分心
calligraphy	[kəˈlɪgrəfɪ]	n.	书法
The Scholar's Four Jewels			文房四宝
black ink			黑墨
Xuan paper			宣纸
thoughtful	[ˈθɔːtfl]	adj.	体贴的

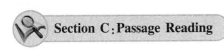

Section C: Passage Reading

Tourism and transportations

In recent years, the Chinese government has encouraged domestic travel and implement a policy of "Holiday Economics", giving its citizens an opportunity to spend more savings on travels, shopping, and eating out. In 2013, total tourist spending was 2.9 trillion RMB.

In 2019, tourism contributed 11.04% of the nation's Gross Domestic Product (GDP), and created 80 million jobs.

China has spent heavily on building roads, railway stations and airports. New airlines and bus companies have emerged, and competition has cut the cost of travel. A one-way air ticket between Shanghai and Beijing costs 850 to 900 yuan, and cheaper prices are occasionally available. Some airlines have begun online ticketing services, making it even easier to take a holiday. More private cars and the emergence of car rental agencies have allowed millions of people to travel on their own, as well as in tour groups.

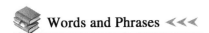

Words and Phrases

encourage	[ɪnˈkʌrɪdʒ]	v.	鼓励
implement	[ˈɪmplɪment]	v.	实施
revenue	[ˈrevənjuː]	n.	税收
estimate	[ˈestɪmət]	v.	估计
investment	[ɪnˈvestmənt]	n.	投资
competition	[ˌkɒmpəˈtɪʃn]	n.	竞争
domestic	[dəˈmestɪk]	adj.	国内的
gross	[grəʊs]	adj.	总的

emerge	[ɪˈmɜːdʒ]	vi.	出现
trillion	[ˈtrɪljən]	n.	万亿
rental	[ˈrentl]	n.	租费

Exercises

Ⅰ. Terms translation

1. domestic travel
2. Holiday Economics
3. Gross Domestic Product
4. one-way air ticket
5. online ticketing services
6. as well as

Ⅱ. Sentence translation

1. In recent years, the Chinese government has encouraged domestic travel and implement a policy of "Holiday Economics", giving its citizens an opportunity to spend more savings on travels, shopping, and eating out.

2. In 2019, tourism contributed 11.04% of the nation's Gross Domestic Product(GDP), and created 80 million jobs.

3. Some airlines have begun online ticketing services, making it even easier to take a holiday.

4. More private cars and the emergence of car rental agencies have allowed millions of people to travel on their own, as well as in tour groups.

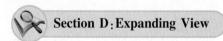

Section D: Expanding View

Electric Multiple Unit

An Electric Multiple Unit or EMU is a Multiple Unit train consisting of many carriages using Electricity as the motive power.

The cars that from a complete EMU set can usually be separated by function into four types: power car, motor car, driving car and trailer car. Each car can have more than one function, such as a motor-driving car or power-driving car.

• Power cars carry the necessary equipment to draw power from the electrified infrastructure, such as contact-shoe device for third rail systems and pantograph for overhead lines systems, and transformers.

• Motor cars carry the traction motor to move the train.

• Driving cars are similar to cab cars, containing a driver's cab for controlling the train. An

Part III/Unit 18 Thanks, Apologies and Advice

EMU usually has two driving cars, with one at each end of the train.

• Trailer cars are any car that carries no traction or power related equipment, and are similar to locomotive-hauled passenger train.

Some of the more famous Electric Multiple Units in the world are high-speed trains: the Shinkansen in Japan, the TGV in France, and the ICE3 in Germany.

EMUs are also popular on commuter and suburban railway networks around the world due to their fast acceleration, pollution free operation and quietness. Being quieter than DMUs (Diesel Multiple Units) and locomotive-hauled trains, EMUs can operate later at night and frequently without disturbing residents living near the railway lines. In addition, tunnel design for EMU trains is simpler as provisions do not need to be made for diesel exhaust fumes.

 Words and Phrases ◀◀◀

Electric Multiple Unit			电动车组
motor	[ˈməʊtə(r)]	n.	马达;发动机
pantograph	[ˈpæntəɡrɑːf]	n.	受电弓
transformer	[trænsˈfɔːmə(r)]	n.	变压器
commuter	[kəˈmjuːtə(r)]	n.	通勤
motive	[ˈməʊtɪv]	adj.	发动的
trailer	[ˈtreɪlə(r)]	n.	拖车
infrastructure	[ˈɪnfrəstrʌktʃə(r)]	n.	基础设施
overhead lines systems			架空线路系统
locomotive-hauled train			机车牵引列车
acceleration	[əkˌseləˈreɪʃn]	n.	加速度

 Section E: Self-evaluation

Ⅰ. Words and phrases translation

1. 自助售票厅

2. 检票口

3. 不得随地吐痰

4. 舱

5. 配备;装配

6. 书法

7. 体贴的

8. 鼓励

9. 实施

10. 竞争

11. 国内的

12. 总的

13. 每年的

14. 电动车组

15. 发动机

16. 拖车

17. 基础设施

18. 变压器

Ⅱ. Sentences translation

1. 抱歉先生,这车是全列禁烟,卫生间也不能吸烟,感谢您的配合!

2. 车速较快,您在车内行走时请注意安全。

3. 您有什么意见或建议?

4. 请接受我诚挚的道歉。

5. 您想喝点什么吗?

6. 您好,列车运行中,请您不要倚靠车门,以免发生危险。

7. 乘车时,不要随意搬动或按下车上的紧急制动阀。

8. 如有需要,请按紧急呼叫按钮。

9. 请不要将杂志带下车。

10. 请您把行李放在行李架上。

Appendix

I. 铁路客运服务词汇

单　　词	音　　标	词性	释　　义
ticket office			售票处
Enquiry Office	[ɪnˈkwaɪərɪ]	n.	问讯处
waiting room			候车室
VIP Watiing Room/VIP Lounge		n.	贵宾室
Time-table			时刻表
ticket office			售票厅
book ticket			订票
Business Class/First class			一等座
First-class berth ticket			一等座软卧票
First-class seat ticket			一等座软座票
Elevator	[ˈelɪveɪtə(r)]	n.	电梯
Luggage storage office			行李寄存处
station hall/station lobby		n.	车站大厅
platform	[ˈplætfɔːm]	n.	站台
Maternal and Infant Waiting Room			母婴候车室
washing room			洗手间
electronic screen	[ɪˌlekˈtrɒnɪk]	adj.	电子屏幕
TVM(Ticket Vending Machine)			自动售票机
refund of ticket		v.	退票
Economy Class /Second Class			二等座
Economy-class seat ticket			二等座硬卧票
Economy-class seat ticket			二等座硬座票
Water Place			饮水处
luggage office			行李托运处
Luggage label	[ˈleɪbl]	n.	行李标签
arrival register			行李登记簿
entrance	[ˈentrəns]	n.	进站口
security check	[sɪˈkjʊərəti]		安检
departure time	[dɪˈpɑːtʃə(r)]		发车时间

续上表

单　词	音　标	词性	释　义
platform-ticket			验票口
ID brush area	[brʌʃ]	v.	身份证识别区
train policeman			乘警
ticket inspector	[ɪnˈspektə(r)]	n.	检票员
crew	[kruː]		乘务组
conductor	[kənˈdʌktə(r)]	n.	男列车员
chief conductor			列车长
dinning car chief			餐车长
compartment	[kəmˈpɑːtmənt]	n.	隔间；包间
middle berth			中铺
ticket check			卧铺牌
charge socket		n.	充电插座
Special Passenger Service			特殊旅客服务
Railway Hotline			铁路客服电话
luggage check			托运单
claim sb's luggage			提取行李
exit	[ˈeksɪt]	n.	出站口
luggage screening machine			行李安检机
Yellow Safety Line			黄色安全线
TCM（Ticket Checking Machine）			自动验票机
automatic face-recognition system		n.	自动人脸识别系统
train announcer			列车广播员
clerk	[klɑːk]	n.	客运员
crew member			乘务人员
conductress	[kənˈdʌktrəs]	n.	女列车员
station master			站长
dinning car attendant			餐车服务员
upper berth			上铺
lower berth			下铺
aisle seat	[aɪl]	n.	过道座位
make a reservation			预定
Railway Customer Service Center of China			中国铁路客户服务中心
handrail	[ˈhændreɪl]	n.	扶手
accessible toilet		adj. n.	无障碍厕所
emergency call button			紧急呼叫按钮

续上表

单词	音标	词性	释义
first aid box			急救箱
accessible toilet			无障碍厕所
baffle gate		n.	闸机
transfer access	[ˈækses]	n.	换乘通道
flush	[flʌʃ]	v.	冲
sensor tap		n.	感应水龙头
Accessible Elevator		adj.	无障碍电梯
Entrance for Special Passengers			重点旅客进站口
magnetic	[mægˈnetik]	adj.	有磁性的
Underground Car Park			地下停车场

Ⅱ. 餐饮词汇

单词	音标	词性	释义
steamed	[stiːmd]	adj.	蒸
quick-fried		adj.	油爆
roast	[rəʊst]	adj.	烤
baked	[beɪkt]	v.	烘焙
scrambled	[skræmbl]	v.	炒
braised in soy sauce			红烧
diced	[ˈdaɪst]	adj.	丁
chunk	[tʃʌŋk]	n.	块
salt	[sɔːlt]	n.	盐
vinegar	[ˈvɪnɪɡə(r)]	n.	醋
ketchup	[ˈketʃəp]	n.	番茄酱
meat	[miːt]	n.	肉
beef	[biːf]	n.	牛肉类
mutton	[ˈmʌtn]	n.	羊肉
ham	[hæm]	n.	火腿
spinach	[ˈspɪnɪtʃ]	n.	菠菜
shrimp	[ʃrɪmp]	n.	虾
fried	[fraɪd]	adj.	油炸的
stewed	[stjuːd]	adj.	炖的
braised	[breɪzd]	adj.	焖的
smoked	[sməʊkt]	adj.	熏的
stir-fry		v.	炒

续上表

单　　词	音　　标	词性	释　　义
sliced	[slaɪs]	adj.	片的
shredded	[ʃred]	adj.	切丝的
ball		n.	丸
sugar	[ˈʃʊɡə(r)]	n.	糖
soy sauce	[ˌsɒɪˈsɔːs]	n.	酱油
pepper sauce	[ˈpepə(r)]	n.	辣椒酱
pork	[pɔːk]	n.	猪肉类
chicken	[ˈtʃɪkɪn]	n.	鸡
duck	[dʌk]	n.	鸭
sausage	[ˈsɒsɪdʒ]	n.	香肠
fish	[fɪʃ]	n.	鱼
cauliflower	[ˈkɒlɪflaʊə(r)]	n.	花菜
cucumber	[ˈkjuːkʌmbə(r)]	n.	黄瓜
carrot	[ˈkærət]	n.	胡萝卜
fungus	[ˈfʌŋɡəs]	n.	木耳
been sprout	[spraʊt]	n.	豆芽
ginger	[ˈdʒɪndʒə(r)]	n.	生姜
eggplant	[ˈeɡplɑːnt]	n.	茄子
Crucian Carp Soup	[ˈkruːʃən] [kɑːp]	n.	鲫鱼汤
Chicken Soup			鸡汤
Vegetable Soup			蔬菜汤
Rice			米饭
Braised Pork Rice			红烧肉饭
Jiaozi / Dumplings			饺子
Baked Scallion Pancake			葱油饼
Sir-fried Noodles			炒面
Hot Dry Noodles			热干面
Sliced Noodles			刀削面
Hot and Sour Rice Noodles			酸辣粉
Congee with Minced Pork and Preserved Egg		n.	皮蛋瘦肉粥
Rice Congee			大米粥
Corn Congee			玉米粥
Salted Duck Egg			咸鸭蛋
celery	[ˈselərɪ]	n.	芹菜

续上表

单 词	音 标	词性	释 义
mushroom	[ˈmʌʃrʊm]	n.	蘑菇
pea	[piː]	n.	青豆
garlic	[ˈgɑːlɪk]	n.	大蒜
shallot	[ʃəˈlɒt]	n.	葱
vegetable	[ˈvedʒtəbl]	n.	蔬菜
Sliced Pork and Mushroom Soup			蘑菇肉片汤
Tomato and Egg Soup			番茄蛋花汤
Laver and Egg Soup			紫菜汤
Fried Rice with egg			蛋炒饭
Steamed Buns			蒸包
Jiaodong Steamed Buns			胶东馒头
Goubu Li Steamed Bread			狗不理包子
Noodles in Soup			汤面
Wonton & Noodles			馄饨和面条
Spicy Hot Noodles			麻辣面
Fried Rice Noodles			河粉
Pumpkin Porridge			南瓜粥
Millet Congee			小米粥
Mung bean Congee			绿豆粥
Spiced Eggs	[spaɪst]	adj.	卤蛋
Steamed Fish			清蒸鱼
Sautéed Slice Pork with Green Pepper			农家小炒肉
Braised Pork Tendons			红烧猪蹄筋
Sauteed Beef with Scallion			葱爆肥牛
Sauteed Shredded Beef in Chili Sauce			干煸牛肉丝
Sauteed Green Chili Pepper			虎皮尖椒
Sauteed Smoked Pork with Chicory			莴笋炒腊肉
Sauteed Pork Mouth with Garlic Sprouts			蒜苗炒猪嘴
beer			啤酒
coffee			咖啡
coffee with cream and sugar			咖啡(加奶,加糖)
tea			茶
green tea			绿茶
yogurt			酸奶
mineral water			矿泉水
Pepsi-Cola			百事可乐

续上表

单　　词	音　　标	词性	释　　义
lemonade			柠檬汁
soda water			汽水
vanilla ice-cream			香草冰激凌
milk-shake			奶昔
Steamed Bass	[beɪs]	n.	清蒸鲈鱼
Sauteed Pork with Black fungus			木耳炒肉片
Liu ning Pork Tendons			流宁猪蹄
Braised Beef Brisket with Tomato			番茄炖牛腩
Sauteed Seasonal Vegetables in Ginger			姜汁炒时蔬
Sauteed Vegetables with Chili Pepper			辣椒炝时蔬
Deep Fried Diced Eggplant with Spicy Salt			椒盐茄子丁
Braised Pork Rib in Soy Sauce			红烧排骨
red wine/port			红葡萄酒/红酒
instant coffee			速溶咖啡
milk			牛奶
black tea			红茶
jasmine tea			茉莉花茶
Coca Cola/coke			可口可乐
Sprite			雪碧
fruit juice			水果汁
orangeade			橘子汁
fresh orange juice			鲜橘子汁
ice candy			冰棒
Haagen-Dazs			哈根达斯

Ⅲ. 火车站

中 文 含 义	英 文 翻 译
进站口/入口	Entrance
检票口	Ticket Check
售票处	Tickets/Booking Office
站台	Platform
出站口/出口	Exit
客运值班室	Passenger Transport Office
请勿乱扔废弃物	Do Not Throw Rubbish

续上表

中 文 含 义	英 文 翻 译
请勿吸烟	No Smoking
凭票候车	Waiting Area for Ticket Holders Only
洗手间	Toilet
饮水处	Drinking Water
重点旅客候车区	Reserved Waiting Room
询问处	Information Office/Enquiry Office
补票处	Pay up on Arrival
男卫生间	Male
女卫生间	Female
无障碍卫生间	Barrier-Free Toilet
吸烟处	Smoking Area
请勿躺卧	Do Not Lie Down
当心滑倒	Caution Slip
小心触电	Danger High Voltage
站台入口	Access to Platforms
行李车	luggage Car/Van/Wagon
行李架	luggage Rack
行李领取处	luggage Delivery Office
行李存放处	luggage Office/Room
行李托运处	luggage Registration Office
小件寄存处	Storage Service(Office)
免费入场	Admission Free
谨防扒手	Beware of Pickpocket
自行车存车处	Bike Parking
公交专用道	Buses Only
营业时间	Business Hours
咖啡馆;小餐馆	Cafe
妇女、儿童优先	Children and Women First
下班	Closed
禁止小便	Commit No Nuisance
意见箱	Complaint Box
危险	Danger
请勿触电	Don't Touch
当心烫伤	Caution Scald Burns
加油站	Filling Station

续上表

中 文 含 义	英 文 翻 译
灭火专用	For Use Only in Case of Fire
易碎	Fragile
快车先行	Give Way
防潮	Guard Against Damp
小心轻放	Handle with Care
置于阴凉处	In Shade
此处插入	Insert Here
切勿近火	Keep Away From Fire
保持干燥	Keep Dry
避光保持	Keep in Dark Place
靠右/左	Keep Right/Left
此面朝上	Keep This Side Up
厕所	Toilet/Washroom
失物招领处	Lost and Found
行李存放处	Luggage Depository
净重	Net Weight
禁止通行	No Admittance
不准张贴	No Bills
禁止携犬入内	No Dogs Allowed
禁止入内	No Entry
(邮政)特快	EMS
请勿拍照	No Photos
(厕所)有人	Occupied
办公时间	Office Hours
对号入座	Seat by Number
紧急求救信号	SOS
员工专用	Staff Only
当心不要丢失东西	Take Care Not to Leave Things Behind
旅行社	Travel Agency
来宾登记	Visitors Please Register
公共大厅	Public Hall
候车室	Waiting Room/Hall
客票	Passenger Ticket
加快票	Fast Extra Ticket
行李托运	luggage Check-in

续上表

中 文 含 义	英 文 翻 译
乘警	Train Policeman
列车广播	Train Broadcasting
发车;出发	Departure
免费运输行李	Free luggage
列车员	Guard
时刻表	Timetable
中铺	Intermediate/Middle Berth
禁止乱扔杂物	No Littering
开车时刻表	Departure Timetable
特快车票	Express Ticket
客快加开票	Fast Extra Passenger Ticket
人行天桥(车站)	Foot Bridge
列车员室	Guard's Compartment
贵宾候车室	Guests' Waiting Room
调车长	Head Shunter
售票站	Issuing Station
软席候车室	Waiting Room for Soft Seat Passengers
行李寄存处	Luggage Storage Service
有效期间(车票)	Period of Availability
站台食品车	Platform Refreshment Trolley
站台地道	Platform Tunnel
邮政车	Postal Car
加快车票	Quick Ticket
退款;退票	Refund, Refund of Ticket
往返票价	Round-trip Fare
服务台	Service Counter
小站	Small Station
车站设备	Station Facilities
站长	Station Master
车站职工	Station Staff
售票员	Ticket Collector
下铺	Lower Berth
上铺	Upper Berth
列车长	Chief Conductor

续上表

中 文 含 义	英 文 翻 译
主任乘务组派班员	Chief Crew-caller
调度长	Chief Dispatcher
小孩票	Child's Ticket Children Ticket
提取行李	Claim Luggage
寄存处(小件行李)	Cloak Room
客车	Coach
冷饮室	Cold-drink Room
中央大厅	Concourse
临时停车	Conditional Halt/Stop
临时列车	Conditional Train
乘务组;乘务人员	Crew
列车乘务人员(美)	Trainman
列车乘务员	Train Staff
无人驾驶列车	Crewless Train
餐车	Dining Car
餐车服务员	Dining Car Attendant
普通加快票	Fast Extra Ticket
豪华客车	Luxury Car
站台商店	Platform Store
提速列车	Plus Speed Train
干线	Principle Line
售票处	Ticket Office/Booking Office
往返车票	Return Ticket
手续费	Service Charge
单层客车	Single-Deck Passenger Coach
车站服务员	Station Attendant
车站餐室	Station Restaurant
车站值班员	Station Operator
车站广场	Station Square
换票证	Ticket Check
查票员	Ticket Inspector
检票口	Ticket Examination Gate
冷藏车	Refrigerator Car/Van/Vehicle/Wagon

IV. 旅游词汇

单　　词	音　　标	词性	释　　义
passport	[ˈpɑːspɔːt]	n.	护照；通行证；手段
rejection	[rɪˈdʒekʃn]	n.	抛弃；拒绝；被抛弃的东西
custom	[ˈkʌstəm]	n.	习惯；惯例；风俗；海关；关税
luggage	[ˈlʌɡɪdʒ]	n.	行李；皮箱
immigrant	[ˈɪmɪɡrənt]	adj.	移民的；迁入的
reunification	[ˌriːjuːnɪfɪˈkeɪʃn]	n.	重新统一；重新团结
visa	[ˈviːzə]	n.	签证
green channel			绿色通道
apply	[əˈplaɪ]	v.	申请；请求
extend	[ɪkˈstend]	v.	延伸；扩大；推广；伸出；给予；使竭尽全力；对……估价；伸展；使疏开
dutiable	[ˈdjuːtiəbl]	adj.	应纳税的；应征税的
article	[ˈɑːtɪkl]	n.	物品；商品
category	[ˈkætəɡəri]	n.	种类；分类
embarkation	[ˌembɑːˈkeɪʃn]	n.	登机；上船
written declaration			书面申报
entry visa			入境签证
red channel			红色通道
contraband	[ˈkɒntrəbænd]	n.	违禁品
valid	[ˈvælɪd]	adj.	有效的
invalid	[ɪnˈvælɪd]	adj.	无效的
expire	[ɪkˈspaɪə(r)]	v.	期满；终止
extend	[ɪkˈstend]	v.	延期
customs duties			进口税
declare	[dɪˈkleə(r)]	v.	申报(应纳税之物)
Oral declaration			口头申报
airport	[ˈeəpɔːt]	n.	机场
plane	[pleɪn]	n.	飞机
flight	[flaɪt]	n.	航班
single/one-way ticket		n.	单程票
return/round-trip ticket		n.	双程票
street			街道
business class			商务舱
speedway	[ˈspiːdweɪ]		高速公路

续上表

单词	音标	词性	释义
turnpike road			收费公路(一般收取通行税)
toll gate			收费站
taxi	[ˈtæksɪ]	n.	出租汽车
cab	[kæb]	n.	出租车
engine	[ˈendʒɪn]	n.	引擎；发动机
coach	[kəʊtʃ]	n.	长途客车
an immigration officer			入境检查员
Transient formalities			过境手续
transit	[ˈtrænzɪt]	v.	过境；换乘
transit card			转机卡
passport inspection			护照检查
customs	[ˈkʌstəmz]	n.	海关；进口税
embassy	[ˈembəsɪ]	n.	大使馆；大使馆全体人员
consulate	[ˈkɒnsjələt]	n.	领事馆
consul	[ˈkɒnsl]	n.	领事
railway station			火车站
subway	[ˈsʌbweɪ]	n.	地铁
underground	[ˌʌndəˈgraʊnd]	n.	地铁
metro	[ˈmetrəʊ]	n.	地铁
highway	[ˈhaɪweɪ]	n.	公路
first class			头等舱
road			公路
economy class			经济舱
vehicle	[ˈviːəkl]	n.	车辆；交通工具机动车
speed limit			速度限制；限速
manual	[ˈmænjʊ(ə)l]	adj.	手动的
automatic	[ɔːtəˈmætɪk]	adj.	自动的
trunk	[trʌŋk]	n.	车后备箱
windshield	[ˈwɪndʃiːld]	n.	风窗玻璃
train	[treɪn]	n.	火车
hotel	[həʊˈtel]	n.	宾馆
inn	[ɪn]	n.	客栈；旅馆
manager	[ˈmænɪdʒə]	n.	经理
housekeeping department			客房部
Food & beverage department			餐饮部
health club			健身房

续上表

单　　词	音　　标	词性	释　　义
room service			客房服务
wake-up call service			叫醒服务
rate	[reɪt]	n.	价格;费用
discount	[ˈdɪskaʊnt]	n.	折扣
tip	[tɪp]	n.	小费
breakfast	[ˈbrekfəst]	n.	早餐;早饭
lunch	[lʌntʃ]	n.	午餐
dinner	[ˈdɪnə]	n.	晚餐;正餐
ketchup	[ˈketʃəp]	n.	番茄酱
chopsticks	[ˈtʃɒpstɪks]	n.	筷子
spoon	[spuːn]	n.	勺子
fork	[fɔːk]	n.	叉;餐叉
knife	[naɪf]	n.	餐刀
dish	[dɪʃ]	n.	盘;餐具;菜肴
bowl	[bəʊl]	n.	碗
napkin	[ˈnæpkɪn]	n.	餐巾,餐巾纸
pork	[pɔːk]	n.	猪肉
beef	[biːf]	n.	牛肉
lamb	[læm]	n.	羔羊肉
mutton	[ˈmʌtn]	n.	羊肉
tire	[taɪə]	n.	轮胎
waiter	[ˈweɪtə]	n.	服务员
waitress	[ˈweɪtrəs]	n.	女服务员
book	[bʊk]	v.	预订;登记
check in			入住登记
check out			结账离开
single room			单人房
double room			双人房
honeymoon suite			蜜月套房
bellboy	[ˈbelbɔɪ]	n.	男侍者;宾馆行李员
receptionist	[rɪˈsepʃənɪst]	n.	前台接待员
chili	[ˈtʃɪli]	n.	辣椒
chili sauce			辣椒酱
soup	[suːp]	n.	汤
main course			主菜
salad	[ˈsæləd]	n.	沙拉

续上表

单　　词	音　　标	词性	释　　义
dessert	[dɪˈzɜːt]	n.	甜点
salt	[sɔːlt]	n.	盐
soy sauce	[sɔɪˈsɔːs]	n.	酱油
vinegar	[ˈvɪnɪgə(r)]	n.	醋
pepper	[ˈpepə]	n.	胡椒
mustard	[ˈmʌstəd]	n.	芥末
Chinese Food			中餐
Western Food			西餐
French Food			法国菜
chicken	[ˈtʃɪkɪn]	n.	鸡肉
spaghetti	[spəˈgetɪ]	n.	意大利式细面条
fish	[fɪʃ]	n.	鱼肉
KFC		n.	肯德基
Pizza Hut		n.	必胜客
Have a nice day.			一天好心情
Have a good day.			祝你愉快！
How do you do?			你好。
How are you?			你好吗?
See you.			再见。
So long.			再见。
See you later.			待会儿见。
See you tomorrow.			明天见。
Take care.			保重。
market	[ˈmɑːkɪt]	n.	市场,集市
supermarket	[ˈsuːpəmɑːkɪt]	n.	超级市场
grocery	[ˈgrəʊsərɪ]	n.	食品杂货店
clothing store			服装店
sporting goods shop			体育用品商店
receipt	[rɪˈsiːt]	n.	收据
invoice	[ˈɪnvɔɪs]	n.	发票
cash	[kæʃ]	n.	现金
cheque	[tʃek]	n.	支票
Credit card	[ˈkredɪt]	n.	信用卡
on fire			着火
gas poisoning			煤气中毒
stroke	[strəʊk]	n.	中风

续上表

单词	音标	词性	释义
barbecue	[ˈbɑːbɪkjuː]	n.	烧烤
fast food		n.	快餐
Mcdonald's	[məkˈdɒnəldz]	n.	麦当劳
Good day!			祝你愉快!
Nice to see you.			见到你很高兴。
Bye-bye.			再见。
Long time no see.			好久不见。
Morning!			早上好!
Good morning!			早上好!
Good afternoon!			下午好!
Good evening!			晚上好!
Good night!			晚安!
department store			百货公司
candy store			糖果店
bookstore	[ˈbʊkstɔː]	n.	书店
florist's	[ˈflɒrɪsts]	n.	花店
optician's	[ɒpˈtɪʃns]	n.	眼镜店
stationer's	[ˈsteɪʃənəs]	n.	文具店
drugstore	[ˈdrʌgstɔː]	n.	药房
pharmacy	[ˈfɑːməsi]	n.	药店
shopping center			购物中心
emergency	[ɪˈmɜːdʒənsi]	n.	紧急情况;突发事件
food poisoning			食物中毒
accidental fire	[ˌæksɪˈdentlˈfæə]		失火
arson	[ˈɑːsn]	n.	纵火,放火
carsickness	[ˈkɑːsɪknəs]	n.	晕车
first-aid	[ˈfəːstˈeɪd]	adj.	急救的;急救用的
ambulance	[ˈæmbjələns]	n.	救护车
stretcher	[ˈstretʃə(r)]	n.	担架
medical worker			医务人员
CPR = cardiopulmonary resuscitation			心肺复苏
smoke	[sməʊk]	n.	烟
burn	[bɜːn]	v.	燃烧;烧毁
scald	[skɔːld]	v.	烫伤
strain	[streɪn]	v.	扭伤
faint	[feɪnt]	vi. & n.	昏倒

续上表

单　　词	音　　标	词性	释　　义
shock	[ʃɒk]	v. & n.	休克
death	[deθ]	n.	死亡
aspirin	[ˈæsprɪn]	n.	阿司匹林
appendicitis	[əˌpendəˈsaɪtɪs]	n.	阑尾炎
fracture	[ˈfræktʃə(r)]	n.	骨折
heart attack			心脏病发作
tour	[tʊə]	n.	旅游；旅行
holiday	[ˈhɒlədeɪ]	n.	假日；节日；休息日
vacation	[vəˈkeɪʃn]	n.	假期
travel agency			旅行社
tour guide			导游
tourist	[ˈtʊərɪst]	n.	旅行者；观光客
low season			淡季
busy season			旺季
travel abroad	[əˈbrɔːd]	adv.	出国旅游
admission ticket			门票
fire alarm			火灾报警器
fire extinguisher	[ˈfaɪərɪkˈstɪŋɡwɪʃə]		灭火器
fire truck			救火车
fire fighter			消防员
hydrant	[ˈhaɪdrənt]	n.	消防栓
fame	[feɪm]	n.	火焰
pill	[pɪl]	n.	药丸
tablet	[ˈtæblɪt]	n.	药片
capsule	[ˈkæpsjuːl]	n.	胶囊
antidote	[ˈæntɪdəʊt]	n.	抗生素
antidote	[ˈæntɪdəʊt]	n.	解毒药
anti-inflammatory	[ˌæntiɪnˈfləˈmətəri]	n.	消炎药
acute disease			急性病
laxative	[ˈlæksətɪv]	n.	轻泻剂
pain-killer		n.	止痛药
penicillin	[ˌpenɪˈsɪlɪn]	n.	青霉素
travel	[ˈtrævl]	v.	旅行
tourist attraction			游览胜地
historic relic			历史古迹
route	[ruːt]	n.	路线

续上表

单词	音标	词性	释义
bridal tour			蜜月旅行
hike	[haɪk]	n.	远足；徒步旅行
family tour			家庭旅行
domestic tour	[dəˈmestɪk]		国内旅游
sightseeing	[ˈsaɪtsiːɪŋ]	n.	观光；游览
voyage	[ˈvɒɪɪdʒ]	n.	航海旅行
place of interest			名胜
accommodation	[əkɒməˈdeɪʃn]		膳宿供应
boat cruise			游船
tourist program			旅游项目
window-shop			（在街上溜达着）看商店橱窗
landscape	[ˈlændskeɪp]		风景
bus tour			巴士观光
kind	[kaɪnd]	n.	种类
a family of three			三口之家
traditional family	[trəˈdɪʃənl]		传统家庭
a happy family			幸福家庭
a farm family			农家
easy-going		adj.	随和的；容易相处的
introvert	[ˈɪntrəvɜːt]	adj.	内向的
extrovert	[ˈekstrəvɜːt]	adj.	外向的
moody	[ˈmuːdi]	adj.	喜怒无常的
ambitious	[æmˈbɪʃəs]		野心勃勃的
conceited	[kənˈsiːtɪd]	adj.	自负的；自以为是的
conservative	[kənˈsɜːvətɪv]	adj.	保守的
first/ given name			名字
nickname	[ˈnɪkneɪm]		外号
Christian name			教名
married	[ˈmærɪd]	adj.	已婚的
single	[ˈsɪŋɡ(ə)l]	adj.	单身的
recommend	[rekəˈmend]	v.	推荐，介绍
sightseeing	[ˈsaɪtsiːɪŋ]	n.	观光；游览
travel brochure	[ˈbrəʊʃə(r)]		旅游手册
tourist attraction	[tuərɪstəˈtrækʃən]		旅游名胜
national park			国家公园
Three-star hotel			三星级酒店

续上表

单　　词	音　　标	词性	释　　义
family	[ˈfæməlɪ]	n.	家庭
considerate	[kənˈsɪdərət]	adj.	体贴的；体谅的
polite	[pəˈlaɪt]	adj.	有礼貌的；客气的
insolent	[ˈɪnsələnt]	adj.	无礼的；傲慢的；粗野的
good-hearted		adj.	好心肠的
a wealthy family			富裕的家庭
a poor family			贫穷的家庭
a high-income family			高收入家庭
a middle-income family			中等收入家庭
A low-income family			低收入家庭
confident	[ˈkɒnfɪdənt]	adj.	自信的；确信的
open-minded	[ˌəʊpənˈmaɪndɪd]	adj.	思想开明的
humorous	[ˈhjuːmərəs]	adj.	诙谐的；幽默的
rude	[ruːd]	adj.	粗鲁的
bad-tempered		adj.	脾气不好的
modest	[ˈmɒdɪst]	adj.	谦虚的
arrogant	[ˈærəgənt]	adj.	自大的，傲慢的
temper	[ˈtempə(r)]	n.	脾气
character	[ˈkærəktə(r)]	n.	性格
attitude	[ˈætɪtjuːd]	n.	态度
console	[kənˈsəʊl]	v.	安慰；慰藉
encourage	[ɪnˈkʌrɪdʒ]	v.	鼓励；怂恿
neutral	[ˈnjuːtrəl]	adj.	中立的
agreement	[əˈgriːmənt]	n.	同意
object	[ˈɒbdʒɪkt]	v.	反对
disagree	[ˌdɪsəˈgriː]	v.	不同意；不一致
disagreement	[ˌdɪsəˈgriːmənt]	n.	不一致；争论
satisfied	[ˈsætɪsfaɪd]	adj.	感到满意的
dissatisfied	[dɪsˈsætɪsfaɪd]	adj.	不满意的；不高兴的
disappointed	[ˌdɪsəˈpɔɪntɪd]	adj.	失望的；沮丧的
support	[səˈpɔːt]	v.	支持
praise	[preɪz]	v.	赞扬；称赞
approve	[əˈpruːv]	adj.	批准；赞成
compliment	[ˈkɒmplɪmənt]	n.	恭维；称赞
blame	[bleɪm]	v.	责备；归咎于
nervous	[ˈnɜːvəs]	adj.	神经的；紧张的

续上表

单词	音标	词性	释义
complain	[kəmˈpleɪn]	v.	抱怨
pessimistic	[ˌpesɪˈmɪstɪk]	adj.	悲观的；厌世的
regretful	[rɪˈgretfʊl]	adj.	后悔的；遗憾的
birthday	[ˈbɜːθdeɪ]	n.	生日；诞辰
toast	[təʊst]	v.	向……祝酒；为……干杯
cheers	[tʃɪəz]	v.	祝贺；鼓励
wedding ceremony	[ˈserəmənɪ]		结婚典礼
stubborn	[ˈstʌbən]	adj.	顽固的；顽强的
timid	[ˈtɪmɪd]	adj.	胆小的；羞怯的
opinion	[əˈpɪnjən]	n.	意见；主张
viewpoint	[ˈvjuːpɔɪnt]	n.	观点
agree	[əˈgriː]	v.	同意
hesitate	[ˈhezɪteɪt]	adj.	踌躇，犹豫
interested	[ˈɪntrəstɪd]	adj.	感兴趣的
indifferent	[ɪnˈdɪfrənt]	adj.	漠不关心的；无关紧要的
patient	[ˈpeɪʃnt]	adj.	有耐心的，能容忍的
impatient	[ɪmˈpeɪʃnt]	adj.	焦躁的；无耐心的
suspect	[səˈspekt]	v.	怀疑
doubtful	[ˈdaʊtfl]	adj.	可疑的
suspicious	[səˈspɪʃəs]	adj.	可疑的；怀疑的
jealous	[ˈdʒeləs]	adj.	妒忌的
anxious	[ˈæŋkʃəs]	adj.	焦虑的；担忧的
worried	[ˈwʌrɪd]	adj.	担心的
criticize	[ˈkrɪtɪsaɪz]	v.	批评；评论
frustrated	[frʌˈstreɪtɪd]	adj.	失意的；挫败的
debase	[dɪˈbeɪs]	v.	降低；使……贬值
optimistic	[ˌɒptɪˈmɪstɪk]	adj.	乐观的
persuade	[pəˈsweɪd]	v.	说服；劝说
dissuade	[dɪˈsweɪd]	v.	劝阻；劝止
happy birthday			生日快乐
birthday present			生日礼物
birthday greetings			生日祝福
birthday cake			生日蛋糕
wedding vow			结婚誓言
wedding ring			结婚戒指
wedding dress			结婚礼服

续上表

单　　词	音　　标	词性	释　　义
marriage certificate			结婚证书
Congratulations！	[kənˌgrætjʊˈleʃənz]		恭喜！
wedding	[ˈwedɪŋ]	*n.*	婚礼；婚宴
wedding dinner			婚宴
groom	[gruːm]	*n.*	新郎
bridesmaid	[ˈbraɪdzmeɪd]		女傧相；伴娘
best man			男傧相；伴郎

Ⅴ．日常用语

日　常　用　语	Everyday Expressions
欢迎你到中国来！	Welcome to China！
欢迎你来到我们的城市！	Welcome to our city！
欢迎你乘坐本次列车！	Welcome to our train！
我很高兴乘坐这次列车！	Glad to take your train！
又见到你很高兴。	Glad to see you again.
好久没见到你了。	Haven't seen you for a long time. / Long time no see.
各位再见！	Goodbye, everybody！
晚安！	Good night！
再见！	See you again. / See you later.
明天见！	See you tomorrow.
希望你以后再来。	Hope you'll come again.
希望你再来中国。	Hope you'll come to China again.
问候你家里人。	Give my best regards to your family. / Please say hello to your family.
希望我们可以再见面。	May we meet again soon?
希望我们不久再见。	I hope we shall meet again soon.
你真好。	It's very kind of you.
谢谢你的帮助。	Thank you for your help.
麻烦你给我买到了车票。	Thank you for the trouble you have taken to get me the ticket.
很对不起。	I'm very sorry. / I'm so sorry. / I'm terribly sorry.
对不起，我不太明白你的意思。	Sorry, I don't quite understand you. / Excuse me, I don't catch your meaning.
对不起，我的英语水平不好，请说慢一点。	Sorry, my English is very poor, please speak more slowly.
请再说一遍好吗？	Pardon?
对不起，请再说一遍。	I beg your pardon. Please say it once more.
对不起，麻烦你一下。	Sorry to trouble you.
对不起，让你久等了。	Sorry to have kept your waiting.

续上表

日 常 用 语	Everyday Expressions
对不起,挡住你的路了。	Sorry to be in your way.
对不起,晚餐还没有好。	Sorry, the supper is not ready.
对不起,水还没有开。	Sorry, the water has not boiled yet.
对我所说的话表示道歉。	I'm sorry for what I've said.
我努力保证这事不再发生。	I'll try to make sure it doesn't happen again.
请告诉我,我去广州该坐哪趟车?	Please tell me which train I should take for Guangzhou.
请在明天早晨7点把我叫醒。	Wake me up at seven tomorrow morning, please.
请告诉我怎样把我的行李运到杭州去好吗?	Will you please tell me how to check my luggage for Hangzhou?
不知道您能否帮我拿一拿行李?	I wander if you could help me with my luggage.
你看来脸色不好。	You look rather pale.
你看来身体不大好。	You don't look well.
你胃口如何?	How is your appetite?
什么时候开始疼的?	When did the pain start?
你不久就会康复的。	You'll be all right soon.
不严重。	It's nothing serious.
没必要惊慌。	There's nothing to be alarmed about.
不要过度疲劳。	Don' overwork yourself.
回家休息至少三四天。	Go home and have rest for at least three or four days.
请给我些碘酒。	Please give me some iodine.
请给我包扎一下。	Wrap it up for me, please.
请赶快给我找个医生来。	Please call a doctor as soon as possible.
请帮忙叫医生好吗?	Would you please call a doctor for me?
医生马上给你检查。	The doctor will examine you in a minute.
要我给你一些止痛药吗?	Shall I get you some pain-killer?
要我给你一些胃痛药吗?	Shall I get you some tablets for stomach-ache?
每4小时服一片。	Take one of these pills every four hours.
每天饭后吃两片,一天吃三次。	Take two tablets three times a day after meal.
给你些碘酒。	Here is some iodine for you.
你最好到医院治疗一下。	You'd better go to hospital for treatment.
要不要我给你找张轮椅来?	Shall I get you a wheel-chair?
请送我到医院。	Please take me to the hospital.
离车站最近的医院在哪里?	Where is the nearest hospital from the station?
你最好在下一站下车到医院去。	You'd better get off the train at the next station and go to hospital.

参 考 文 献

[1] 王慧.高铁客运英语口语[M].成都:西南交通大学出版社,2015.
[2] 潘自影.铁路客运英语[M].成都:西南交通大学出版社,2018.
[3] 王渊龙.高速铁路客运服务英语口语[M].成都:西南交通大学出版社,2018.
[4] 王越.铁路旅客运输服务[M].北京:人民交通出版社股份有限公司,2017.
[5] 梁伟.高速铁路实用英语口语[M].北京:中国铁道出版社,2013.
[6] 北京铁路局.高铁车站客运实用英语[M].北京:中国铁道出版社,2011.
[7] 伍帅英,应婷婷.轨道交通英语口语实训教程[M].大连:大连理工大学出版社,2015.
[8] 张莉.铁路客运服务英语口语[M].上海:上海交通大学出版社,2015.
[9] 陈薇薇.新实用城市轨道交通英语口语教程[M].北京:北京交通大学出版社,2017.
[10] 刘慧,应婷婷.新潮轨道交通英语口语教程[M].北京:商务印书馆,2019.